SpringerBriefs in Information Systems

Series editor
Jörg Becker

More information about this series at http://www.springer.com/series/10189

Thomas Fischer • René Riedl

Lifelogging for Organizational Stress Measurement

Theory and Applications

Springer

Thomas Fischer
University of Applied Sciences
Upper Austria
Steyr, Austria

René Riedl
University of Applied Sciences
Upper Austria
Steyr, Austria

Johannes Kepler University Linz
Linz, Austria

ISSN 2192-4929 ISSN 2192-4937 (electronic)
SpringerBriefs in Information Systems
ISBN 978-3-319-98710-1 ISBN 978-3-319-98711-8 (eBook)
https://doi.org/10.1007/978-3-319-98711-8

Library of Congress Control Number: 2018955395

This Springer imprint is published by the registered company Springer Nature Switzerland AG
The registered company address is: Gewerbestrasse 11, 6330 Cham, Switzerland

Contents

Lifelogging for Organizational Stress Measurement: Theory and Applications

1 Introduction

Since the original research report by Hans Selye in the 1930s (Selye, 1936), stress has been an important research topic, predominantly due to its possible detrimental effects ("strains") on individual well-being and health, as well as its negative effects on organizations and society. Among others, Cooper and Cartwright (1994) highlighted that "healthy organizations" must not only be characterized by their financial success, but should consider the health of the individuals working in the organization, for example indicated by high individual job satisfaction and low labor turnover rates. Goh, Pfeffer, and Zenios (2015) estimated the costs and deaths in the US caused by work-related stress based on eight factors (e.g., work hours and shift work, job control and job demands, social support). They report that 5–8% of the US national health care expenditures (about US$174 billion) and about 120,000 annual deaths can be attributed to work-related stress. Thus, work is a main source of most individuals' daily levels of stress (e.g., Anderson et al., 2015), and therefore exploring the mechanisms of *organizational stress* (hereafter: OS) is pivotal.

Independent of the specific research area and the concrete research question, stress researchers studying cause/effect-relationships are concerned with the development and test of theoretical models in which they hypothesize the relationship between different constructs (based on Edwards & Bagozzi, 2000, p. 155, we define a construct as "a conceptual term used to describe a phenomenon of theoretical interest"). As most constructs in OS research cannot be observed directly, their operationalization and the development of appropriate measurement instruments are key activities in the research process. Prior OS research has applied various instruments, predominantly methods and tools from social science research (interview and survey, e.g., Cavanaugh, Boswell, Roehling, & Boudreau, 2000; Pearlin, 1989; Weiss, 1983) and endocrinological research (measurement of stress hormones

T. Fischer, R. Riedl, *Lifelogging for Organizational Stress Measurement*,
SpringerBriefs in Information Systems,
https://doi.org/10.1007/978-3-319-98711-8_1

such as adrenaline, noradrenaline, or cortisol, e.g., Emurian, 1993; Evans & Johnson, 2000; Frese, 1985). Yet, despite the long tradition of OS research, scholars in this domain still face a number of significant measurement challenges.

First, there are a number of methods that can be employed to *capture* specific elements of the stress process (e.g., surveys to capture perceptions, observations to capture behavior, or neurophysiological measures to capture bodily reactions). Each method has advantages and disadvantages (Kahn & Byosiere, 1992; Kasl, 1978; Sonnentag & Frese, 2013). Hence, instead of choosing one method only, the combination of methods (i.e., multi-method or even mixed-method approaches, see Venkatesh, Brown, & Bala, 2013; Venkatesh, Brown, & Sullivan, 2016) has repeatedly been suggested to balance the methods' individual advantages and disadvantages, while also allowing for triangulation of data, thus creating a more complete picture of the stress process (Perrewé & Zellars, 1999). Yet, the implementation of a multi-method or mixed-method approach can be difficult from a data collection perspective (e.g., subjects feel overwhelmed, a fact that holds particularly true in field studies, e.g., Venkatesh et al., 2013, 2016).

Second, the combination of methods is essential due to the sheer number of constructs that are involved in the OS process. In addition to individual capabilities and organizational demands, researchers interested in OS cannot simply limit their efforts to the physical confines of an organization (Kahn & Byosiere, 1992; Kasl, 1978). Instead, it is necessary to also measure factors (i.e., at least to control for them) external to the organization as potential sources of stress that can spill over to the organizational context (e.g., work-home conflict, financial problems, or external commitments, Beehr & Newman, 1978; Cooper & Cartwright, 1994; Danna & Griffin, 1999; Parker & DeCotiis, 1983). Hence, measurement instruments should accompany subjects in as many situations of their daily live as possible and, instead of only focusing on a very limited number of specific constructs of interest, researchers should attempt to capture many, or even most, of an individual's daily experiences. Based on such a rich dataset, analytical techniques can be used to make inferences about constructs of interest, a process that is commonly referred to as *information retrieval.*

The third measurement challenge is related to the *dynamic aspects of stress.* Lazarus (1990), for example, pointed to the importance of measuring as close to the occurrence of stress encounters as possible, particularly when utilizing self-report measures (e.g., due to memory distortion). Indeed, several studies have found that human memory can be quite fallible (e.g., Kelly et al., 2011; Vemuri & Bender, 2004), and, based on the understanding of stress as a dynamic concept, only collecting data at one point in time would lead to limited insights on its sources and effects, as well as the unfolding of stress over time. Hence, a more frequent use of longitudinal study designs has been emphasized in OS research during the past decades (e.g., Edwards, 1992; Frese & Zapf, 1988; Kahn & Byosiere, 1992; Kasl, 1978; Riedl, 2013; Sonnentag & Frese, 2013). Yet, for many reasons it can (still) be a challenge to apply a longitudinal research design to stress research (e.g., obtrusiveness of measurement routines and amounts of created data) and hence it is not

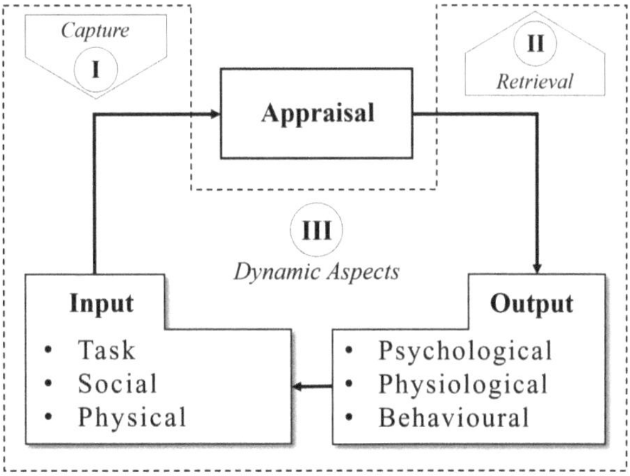

Fig. 1 Conceptual framework of stress and proposed contributions of lifelogging

surprising that there are a number of methodological limitations in current research that require novel measurement approaches.

In order to cope with these major challenges, a research opportunity for OS researchers has emerged in the form of *lifelogging* in recent years. This concept is based on the idea that unobtrusive computer technology can be used to continuously collect data on an individual's current state (psychological, physiological, or behavioral) and context (ranging from ambient temperature, to information on human social interaction, and human interaction with information and communication technologies). Particularly, lifelogging has the goal of enabling an individual to collect the totality of his or her experiences through the digitization of all cognitive inputs (Dodge & Kitchin, 2007) in a way that requires little effort and that is complete in terms of data (i.e., capturing a whole lifetime of experiences, Sellen & Whittaker, 2010). Therefore, lifelogging is concerned with the longitudinal capture and processing of a large amount and variety of data and hence may be well suited to aid in overcoming some of the more persistent challenges in OS research.

In the present book, we aim to substantiate this observation and discuss how the concept of lifelogging may contribute to construct measurement in longitudinal OS research, as a potential complement to existing measurement approaches. For this purpose, we base our investigation on the contemporary understanding of stress as an interaction between the individual and the environment, as proposed in the transactional theory of stress (e.g., Lazarus, 1966; Lazarus & Folkman, 1984). The remainder of this book is structured along the focal domains of stress as highlighted in Fig. 1 (within the dashed line; note that we do not focus on individual appraisal processes per se as they cannot be directly assessed, but instead can only be approximated through the assessment of relevant inputs and consequential outputs) and the main challenges for OS research we have highlighted (represented numerically in Fig. 1). First, we discuss the main types of constructs involved in the OS process (Sect. 2). Based on this conceptual foundation, we discuss lifelogging in greater detail and present the results of a descriptive review of landmark lifelogging publications as well as state-of-the-art lifelogging research, which substantiates the potential of lifelogging for OS research (Sect. 3). In the final section we will then summarize our discussion and draw conclusions on the potential of lifelogging for OS research.

2 Constructs in Organizational Stress Research

Lazarus (1990) suggested that, in a theory-driven approach to the measurement of stress, the most important facets of the stress process should be measured, which he broke down into (1) the content of daily stressful encounters (which would correspond to "Input" in Fig. 1) and (2) the intensity of stressful reactions ("Output"), as well as (3) the fluctuations of inputs and outputs, and their relationships, over time. Particularly, most theories of OS follow the basic cybernetic principle of a feedback loop (e.g., as shown by Edwards, 1992) to combine all three of these facets of stress (e.g., stress perceptions as inputs guiding coping behaviors as outputs, which lead to changes of the current situation and thus new inputs for perception, and so forth). It follows that adopting a cybernetic approach to the study of stress implies the application of a longitudinal research perspective (Cummings & Cooper, 1979; Edwards, 1992). This major categorization of constructs as inputs or outputs in the OS process will also guide our overview of the main types of constructs that could be informed through lifelogging data.

2.1 Constructs on the Input Side

On the "Input" side of the stress process we include all aspects of the environment that are perceived by the individual. Basically, all stimuli perceived throughout a workday and even beyond (e.g., e-mails checked after official hours) could have an impact on appraisal processes (Lazarus & Folkman, 1984). What we conceptualize as "Input" side in our model in Fig. 1 is often referred to as *context* in organizational behavior studies, defined as "any information that can be used to characterize the situation of an entity" (Dey, 2001, p. 5). In the extant literature a number of constructs are described which make up the context. These constructs constitute potential inputs for the OS process. Specifically, in the present article we adopt a two-level classification of contextual variables proposed by Johns (2006).

The first level, the *omnibus context*, focuses on the wider understanding of a situation and comprises five main questions that should be answered (i.e., Who? What? When? Where? Why?). The second level, the *discrete context*, focuses on the particular situation and therefore includes three dimensions related to the organizational environment itself, namely (1) task context, (2) social context, and (3) physical context. While the omnibus context can be a first step in describing a situation, we are more interested in the situational details that lead to stress and, accordingly, focus on the three dimensions in the discrete context. Similar classifications have frequently been employed in OS research to classify potential stressors (e.g., Beehr & Newman, 1978; Cooper & Cartwright, 1994; Kahn & Byosiere, 1992; McGrath, 1976; Sonnentag & Frese, 2013).

In the *task context* we include constructs which are related to (a) the characteristics of the job itself (e.g., task complexity and workload) and their (b) organization and development over time (e.g., work organization and decision latitude), as well as (c) demands that can arise from outside of one's formal job functions, particularly from perceptions of an individual's role(s) in the organization (e.g., role conflict and role ambiguity). In the *social context* we include constructs which are related to the (a) social interactions with other individuals in an organization (e.g., conflicts at work), as well as elements which are, in a wider sense, the (b) result of individual interactions on an organizational level (e.g., organizational climate). In the *physical context* we include constructs which are directly related to the (a) physical and technological circumstances at work (e.g., faulty equipment), but also constructs which are associated with the (b) direct results of these organizational circumstances (e.g., potential for safety hazards through overcrowding).

2.2 Constructs on the Output Side

On the "Output" side, three dimensions are most widely acknowledged, including constructs on the psychological, physiological, and behavioral levels (e.g., Beehr & Newman, 1978; Frese & Zapf, 1988; Kahn & Byosiere, 1992; Sonnentag & Frese, 2013).

In addition to strains (i.e., negative effects of stress), Lazarus (1990) argued that adjustment processes (i.e., efforts to counter stress) are an integral part of the output side of stress. OS stress research focuses on consciously controlled adjustment processes; hence, adaptations on the physiological level alone (i.e., homeostasis) are not considered in our model.

On the *psychological level*, we include constructs that are (a) directly or indirectly related to an individual's mental well-being (e.g., negative affective reactions) and effects that can, at least indirectly, be a (b) threat to organizational well-being (e.g., reduced organizational commitment). For coping, we focus on (c) emotion-related efforts to reduce the effects of stress (e.g., acceptance of the situation). On the *physiological level* we focus on constructs that can be inferred from changes in physiological functioning (e.g., changes in blood pressure, heart rate, hormone secretion, Carayon, Smith, & Haims, 1999; Kahn & Byosiere, 1992), indicative of (a) acute stress (e.g., affective states such as anger, indicated by changes in body temperature) or (b) the potential longitudinal effects of chronic exposure to stressors (e.g., risk of cardiovascular disease indicated by reduced heart rate variability or increased blood pressure). On the *behavioral level*, we apply a conceptual distinction between (a) the behavioral consequences of stress, being less open to direct control and active decision-making (e.g., addictive behaviors such as a compulsion to smoke in stressful situations) and (b) the behaviors to deal with stress (i.e., coping behaviors, such as seeking social support).

2.3 Methodological Limitations

To provide a systematic account of the main limitations of OS research applying longitudinal designs, particularly pertaining to the three main measurement challenges discussed in the Introduction, we conducted a literature review. Importantly, two decades ago, Zapf, Dormann, and Frese (1996) already presented a review of longitudinal OS studies in which they highlighted the common challenges for research at their time, such as the difficulty of choosing adequate time lags between measurement points or the difficulty of measuring all relevant variables at each point of data collection. We continued the work of Zapf and colleagues and reviewed studies which have been published since then.

For this purpose we used the combination "Stress" (Topic) AND "Organization*" (Topic) AND "Longitudinal" (Topic) to search for suitable journal publications in "Web of Science"; we conducted our last search on 08/25/2016. We excluded studies which do not focus on OS in a wider sense (i.e., focusing at least on one input and output construct), did not collect any data, or were not longitudinal in nature, and ended up with 130 publications. Out of these publications we chose the 50 articles published in the highest-impact journals (i.e., 2-year impact factor of at least 3), including, amongst others, the most prestigious management journals such as the Academy of Management Journal, Journal of Management, or the Journal of Organizational Behavior (for further details, please refer to Sect. 1 in the chapter "Appendix").

We reviewed the limitations that have been highlighted in these studies and identified five main areas that are of particular interest for construct measurement. It has to be noted though, that we do not include limitations here that can be mainly attributed to the specific hypotheses (e.g., variables that have been measured and additional variables that could be measured) or the specific samples that have been selected (e.g., limited generalizability of the results due to a specific organizational context).

In Table 1, we list the five main areas of limitations we identified and indicate to which of the three main challenges in OS research we attribute them. Also, we list exemplary studies and selected limitation statements.

In "Limited Capture" we include limitations mainly pertaining to the limits of the data collection routines in capturing constructs of interest (e.g., behaviors outside of the organization). In "Types of Measures" we include limitations pertaining to the methods of data collection, such as self-reports entailing the risk of common method bias and limiting researchers mostly to the subjective capture of constructs (e.g., perceived workload, instead of actual workload). In "Sample Characteristics" we include limitations pertaining to the study design, but also properties of data collection instruments, not allowing for the inclusion of subjects with pronounced

Table 1 Main methodological limitations in longitudinal OS research

Type of Limitation	Exemplary Limitation Statements
Limited Capture (*Capture*, see Fig. 1) Exemplary Studies: Bono, Glomb, Shen, Kim, and Koch (2013); Bragard, Etienne, Merckaert, Libert, and Razavi (2010); Childs and Stoeber (2012); Ilies, Schwind, Wagner, and Johnson (2007)	"Because we used spousal ratings of employees' behaviors, the social behaviors that we assessed in the family domain had to be limited to activities that could be rated by the participants' spouses. However, many other behaviors and activities in the family domain such as exercising, reading, and working on hobbies are relevant to employees' well-being (. . .)." (Ilies et al., 2007) "Missed assessments were largely due to scheduling difficulties and staff being on vacation at the time of data collection (. . .)." (Steptoe et al., 1998, p. 90)
Types of Measures (*Capture*, see Fig. 1) Exemplary Studies: Brennan, Chugh, and Kline (2002); Edwards, Guppy, and Cockerton (2007); Idris, O'Driscoll, and Anderson (2011); Moen, Kelly, and Lam (2013)	"[A] limitation of the study was the lack of objective measures. All the data gathered were strictly based on self-reports of employee perceptions of performance and satisfaction." (Brennan et al., 2002, p. 295) "(. . .) health outcomes were all self-reported; future research is necessary to test the effects of changes in time strain measures on more objective health outcomes." (Moen et al., 2013, p. 166)
Sample Characteristics (*Capture*, see Fig. 1) Exemplary Studies: Ilies et al. (2007); Nielsen and Randall (2012); Pas, Bradshaw, and Hershfeldt (2012); Van der Elst et al. (2014)	"(. . .) workers with high levels of turnover intentions may actually have changed jobs and thus left the organization compared to workers with low levels of turnover intentions." (Van der Elst et al., 2014, p. 160) "(. . .) drop-out analyses indicated that employees who responded both times experienced higher job satisfaction and affective well-being. A healthy worker effect may have influenced our findings in that only healthy workers responded to the questionnaire both times." (Nielsen & Randall, 2012, p. 106)
Data Analysis (*Information Retrieval*, see Fig. 1) Exemplary Studies: Amiot, Terry, Jimmieson, and Callan (2006); Biggs, Brough, and Barbour (2014); Petrou, Demerouti, and Schaufeli (2015); Stiglbauer, Selenko, Batinic, and Jodlbauer (2012)	"(. . .) future studies could test if a curvilinear relation exists between stress and employee adjustment and whether a specific amount of stress could actually be beneficial during organizational change (i.e., eustress)." (Amiot et al., 2006, p. 568) "(. . .) our two wave design does not enable us to fully address mediating relationships because that would entail a three-wave design whereby every variable of the relationship is measured within a different wave." (Petrou et al., 2015, p. 477)

(continued)

Table 1 (continued)

Type of Limitation	Exemplary Limitation Statements
Points and Lag (*Dynamic Aspects*, see Fig. 1) Exemplary Studies: Bono et al. (2013); Hyvonen, Feldt, Kinnunen, and Tolvanen (2011); Reknes et al. (2014); Sanchez and Viswesvaran (2002)	"In essence, measurement stability over time may not matter when the causal lag between stressors and strains is not adequately captured by the timing of the measurement." (Sanchez & Viswesvaran, 2002, p. 180) "24-hour monitoring might aid in understanding the role of time in links between work events, stress, and health, as would jointly examining a diverse set of physiological measures (e.g., both blood pressure and cortisol)." (Bono et al., 2013, p. 1621)

strain (e.g., subjects that have left the organization due to clinical burnout), but also resignation of participants due to additional measurement effort (e.g., keeping a diary despite the fact that workload is already high). In "Data Analysis" we include limitations pertaining to information retrieval, such as specific types of relationships between constructs that could additionally be tested (e.g., non-linear relationships or reversed causations), and particularly the limited possibility to test mediation effects (because most studies only use two points of data collection). Finally, and most often referenced in reviewed studies, in "Points and Lag" we include limitations pertaining to the chosen number of measurement points and the lags between them, with several studies highlighting that continuous measurement over a longer duration would be ideal, though it would likely also entail too much effort for both researchers and participants.

3 Lifelogging

To support construct measurement in longitudinal OS research, we propose lifelogging as an additional research avenue in this section. For this purpose, we first introduce the notion of lifelogging and then discuss what type of data we can capture using lifelogging tools and practices, which inferences have commonly been made from it, and how this can contribute to construct measurement in longitudinal OS research. We base this discussion on the previously presented review of the methodological limitations that have been highlighted in longitudinal OS studies, as well as on a review of landmark lifelogging publications and state-of-the-art lifelogging research.

3.1 Background and Vision of Lifelogging

A lifelog is the result of continuous self-tracking efforts and can be defined as "(. . .) a form of pervasive computing consisting of a unified digital record of the totality of an individual's experiences, captured multimodally through digital sensors and stored permanently as a personal multimedia archive" (Dodge & Kitchin, 2007, p. 431). Initially envisioned by Vannevar Bush (1945), the creation of such a digital archive (or even an extended memory) has become a reality due to technological developments (e.g., sensor and storage capabilities of devices). For example, Gordon Bell, a well-known electrical engineer, uses a system called "MyLifeBits" (Bell, 2001; Gemmell, Bell, & Lueder, 2006) to collect all sorts of documents, with the goal of a paperless environment.

A major reason why lifelogging could significantly advance construct measurement in future OS research is that lifelogging can easily become a regular activity of many people worldwide and it does not involve a significant change of daily behaviors and routines. In a 2013 survey, 69% of the participants (nationwide survey of 3014 adults in the US) already reported that they are regularly keeping track of at least one health indicator (e.g., diet or weight), of which 21% used technology to support this endeavor (Fox & Duggan, 2013), and in a 2014 survey (465 individuals and 134 researchers in the US) the share of self-trackers in the US was already 91% (California Institute for Telecommunications and Information Technology, 2014).

What supports this development is the fast-paced diffusion of high-performance personal technologies, with mobile devices, particularly smartphones, presenting an exceptional opportunity for lifelogging (Li, Dey, & Forlizzi, 2012). Being highly prevalent, with an estimated two billion units being shipped in 2016 alone (Gartner, 2015), mobile devices offer increasing sensory performance and storage capabilities (Gurrin, Smeaton, & Doherty, 2014), thereby technologically paving the way for the continuing dissemination of lifelogging.

Academic research has also started to develop insights into the nature, antecedents, and consequences of the lifelogging phenomenon (Gurrin et al., 2014), particularly into the potential of lifelogging technologies for the study of health-related phenomena. Czerwinski et al. (2006), for example, highlighted that a large set of individual-level data created through lifelogging could be pooled together, which would allow for better examination of organizational phenomena. Also, Bell and Gemmell (2009) emphasized the creation of individual-level data as a basis for epidemiological research, highlighting the potential of lifelogging for inferences on higher levels of analysis, particularly the societal level (e.g., as input for stress cost estimations, see Goh et al., 2015).

Importantly, the collection of personal data through technological means also allows for a more objective approach to the identification of stress sources and stress measurement, as individuals are, at least sometimes, prone to experience difficulties when identifying stress sources and/or reporting the level of their own stress (e.g., Cooper & Cartwright, 1994; Riedl, 2013). Recently, it has been demonstrated that "physiological stress measurement explains and predicts variance in performance on a computer-based task over and above the prediction afforded by a self-reported stress measure" (Tams et al., 2014, p. 723). This result suggests that use of both measures together provides a better understanding than does either one alone. Generally, through lifelogging new avenues of field research in organizational environments open up, enabling advanced studies of the dynamic aspects of stress.

3.2 Contributions of Lifelogging to Organizational Stress Research

In order to discuss the potential contributions of lifelogging to construct measurement in longitudinal OS research, we conducted a review of the lifelogging literature (see Sect. 2 in chapter "Appendix").

First, in order to assess which *types of data* have traditionally received high interest in lifelogging research (informing "*Capture*", Fig. 1), we conducted a descriptive review of landmark publications in this domain (Paré, Trudel, Jaana, & Kitsiou, 2015). These publications do not necessarily represent the state-of-the-art of the entire research domain, yet they constitute a useful basis to gain insights into the field and the major types of data which have been collected regularly in existing research. For this purpose, we selected a total of 69 journal publications based on a search in Google Scholar (term: Lifelog*; date: 06/01/2017; hits: 5750).

Second, as *information retrieval* is a main challenge in current lifelogging research and development efforts, we extended the review (informing "*Retrieval*", Fig. 1). This extension involved a forward search using the 69 landmark publications as input (Source: Google Scholar; date: 07/05/2017; combined citations: 4299), which gave us access to more recent journal and conference publications, and reduced the threat of a bias towards older publications (for methodological details of this approach, see Boell & Cecez-Kecmanovic, 2014). We focused on those publications which used data captured with off-the-shelf devices (e.g., mobile phones, fitness trackers, smartwatches), resulting in the selection of 86 publications, representing the state-of-the-art in lifelogging. The reason why we focus on off-the-shelf devices is that they are available to *all* researchers, while proprietary devices are not (see the section "Devices Used for Capture" further below, for details).

Publications related to "Capture" and "Retrieval" inform how lifelogging fosters the handling of the *dynamic aspects* of OS on a micro level (e.g., detection of state changes through analyses of temporal consistency in physiological parameters, Byrne, Doherty, Snoek, Jones, & Smeaton, 2010) and on a macro level (e.g., inference of lifestyle patterns, Doherty et al., 2011). For this purpose, we combined the sample of studies (i.e., 69 plus 86 publications) and focused on those studies which captured data on a longitudinal basis (i.e., we included studies which captured data on more than 1 day; 36 out of 69 studies in the first sample and 49 out of 86 studies in the second sample).

Table 2 Overview of types of data captured for lifelogging research

N (Studies)	Individual	Environment	Device-Specific	Third-Party
69	34	65	19	7
Main Sources	Motion (24) Physiology (4)	Visual (40) Location (23) Audio (15)	Calls (8) Wifi (8) Photos (4)	Weather information (5) Web sources (3)

3.2.1 Data Capture

As the types of data captured for the purpose of lifelogging can be almost limitless (e.g., Gurrin et al., 2014; Wang & Smeaton, 2013), we employed a categorization used by Jacquemard, Novitzky, O'Brolcháin, Smeaton, and Gordijn (2014) to divide them into four main groups. The first category represents "inward facing" data, which we refer to as "*individual*" data in the current article (in order to align terminology with that used in stress research). Data in this category concerns the individual as the object of interest (e.g., data on movements or physiological functioning). The second category, referred to as "*environment*" data (originally "outward facing" data), refers to the capture of an individual's surroundings (e.g., visual impressions and sounds). The third category of "*device-specific*" data focuses on technological devices such as a smartphone and their functioning (e.g., received phone calls or used applications). The fourth category, "*third-party*" data, includes all sorts of information that can be requested from others (e.g., data on the individual from medical providers, weather information, or data from web services for geolocation purposes).

As shown in Table 2, the extant lifelogging literature has a focus on environmental and individual data. Moreover, our analysis of studies reveals that the capture of visual data is the main source of data in the "environment" category, while the capture of movements is the main source of data in the "individual" category.

Types of Data Captured

The by far most popular source of *data on the individual* in the reviewed publications was motion, measured via accelerometers. For example, Blum, Pentland, and Troster (2006) employed accelerometer data to infer individual postures or physical activities (e.g., sitting, standing or walking). Abe, Morinishi, Maeda, Aoki, and Inagaki (2009), to state another example, presented an approach to infer the transportation mode (walk, car, train) of an individual from accelerometer data as an alternative to GPS-inferred changes in location.

With the exception of four studies, an individuals' physiological signals have not been captured frequently in lifelogging research thus far. This result is a surprise because lifelogging holds great potential to offer insight into phenomena of which the individual is not consciously aware (e.g., Bell & Gemmell, 2007; Dodge & Kitchin, 2007). Ryoo and Bae (2007), Brindley, Bateman, and Gracey (2011), and

Ivonin, Chang, Chen, and Rauterberg (2013) included physiological sensors in their studies which can be used to measure cardiovascular signals (heart rate and heart rate variability) in order to make psychophysiological inferences (e.g., stress levels or mental states derived from physiological indicators). Smith, Frost, Albayrak, and Sudhakar (2007) featured the measurement of blood glucose for self-management of diabetes patients.

Environmental data are used to capture the context of individuals. Context information is of paramount importance to understanding stress levels in organizational settings (Johns, 2006). Visual lifelogs are by far the most prominent data type in this category and in many cases the SenseCam was used for data capture (the SenseCam is a wearable camera device which can easily amass thousands of pictures over a short period of time with a default setting of one picture taken every 30 s, which can result in almost 3000 pictures over the course of 24 hours, Hodges, Berry, & Wood, 2011).

Despite their less frequent application in lifelogging research, there are also other useful types of environmental data, such as audio or location data. For example, Vemuri and Bender (2004) as well as Blum et al. (2006) captured audio data and used speech recognition to infer moments which are likely more memorable to the individual. From a stress perspective, it is important to indicate that evidence shows that people speak with a higher pitch and with more variation in pitch when under increased arousal or stress (Bachorowski & Owren, 1995; Hansen, 1996; Juslin & Scherer, 2005; Nunamaker, Derrick, Elkins, Burgoon, & Patton, 2011). It follows that audio data capture along with application of corresponding data analysis algorithms, at least in some organizational situations, may reveal insight into stress levels. Another interesting application with significant relevance to OS research is described in Whittaker, Tucker, Swampillai, and Laban (2008). They compared a number of systems that could be used to capture meetings and showed that captured audio data are amongst the most often used sources to infer social interactions in meetings (e.g., including recognition of who is speaking, when there is discourse between speakers, and transcripts of what has been said). Because social interaction among individuals can both increase (e.g., conflicts in meetings) and decrease (e.g., praising employees) stress, the systems described in Whittaker et al. (2008) may constitute a viable technological basis for OS research.

Location, in this context mostly inferred from GPS data, has also been a valuable data source in a number of lifelogging publications (e.g., Cho, Kim, Hwang, & Song, 2007; Doherty & Smeaton, 2010; Hwang & Cho, 2009; Ryoo & Bae, 2007). Location data can, for example, be used to infer an individual's mode of transportation (Abe et al., 2009), which could be informative of the daily level of physical activity (e.g., commuting to work with the car, bike, or on foot) and the effort required to even come to work (e.g., an hour of commute to work is a likely stressor for most individuals).

Capture of *device-specific data* mainly covers the status of a device and its interactions with the user or other users and their devices. For example, lifelogging pioneer Gordon Bell used the extended memory application "MyLifeBits" also to keep track of his interactions with digital objects and electronic devices. Specifically, interaction with digital files (e.g., electronic documents, e-mails, or multimedia files), as well as hardware and software (e.g., use of peripherals such as mouse and keyboard or application software) can inform stress investigations (Barley, Meyerson, & Grodal, 2011; Gemmell et al., 2006; Riedl, 2013) because IT use is a major source of work stress.

Device-specific data has been of particular importance in the context of studies that used mobile phones as the main device for data capture. A wide variety of data has been collected, such as calls made and received, interaction with installed applications, or music listened to (e.g., Cho et al., 2007; Gurrin, Qiu, et al., 2013; Hwang & Cho, 2009). Moreover, social interactions were inferred from proximity of other smartphones with activated Bluetooth (Gurrin, Qiu, et al., 2013).

Only five studies also retrieved *data from third parties*, particularly from web sources, which are not directly related to the individual, but can be used to enrich an individual's lifelog. For example, aiming to combine visual and location data, Doherty and Smeaton (2010) retrieved images from online photo sharing services (e.g., Flickr) to enhance a visual lifelog of interesting places with the perspectives of other users who had visited the same place. Also, Vemuri and Bender (2004), Cho et al. (2007) and Hwang and Cho (2009) gathered weather information from local institutions to create a richer picture of the daily circumstances.

Devices Used for Capture

In the 69 landmark publications, mostly *mobile devices* (in contrast to ambient sensing) have been used to capture data. We classified these devices as "off-the-shelf" (i.e., consumer-grade devices which can be bought off the shelf and hence are easily available for OS researchers) or "proprietary" (i.e., devices, or combinations of sensors, which are, at least in part, self-developed or modified for the specific study purpose).

We found that two thirds of the studies (51 out of 69) had employed off-the-shelf devices, of which 24 used mobile phones for data collection and 20 used the SenseCam. Aside from more elaborate setups relying on a combination of sensing devices (e.g., McDuff, Karlson, Kapoor, Roseway, & Czerwinski, 2012), Gurrin, Smeaton, Qiu, and Doherty (2013) highlighted that "[t]he ideal device would include sensors that can capture a rich life-experience archive, not impose an additional user burden by bringing/wearing additional devices, operate all day without requiring additional power sources, have onboard storage and support real-time communication." (p. 70). They also created an extensive list of features that indicate that *mobile phones* could be classified as such "ideal devices", including their sensory capabilities, data processing capabilities, continuous improvement of software, ubiquity, self-efficacy of users, and their low cost. As can be expected, mobile phones were far more prevalent amongst the studies included in the second stage of our review, which only focused on off-the-shelf devices, with 50 out of 86 studies applying them for data capture.

Table 3 Main off-the-shelf tools used for data collection in reviewed lifelogging studies

Devices and exemplary studies	Description/devices
Autographer[a] (environmental data) Kelly et al. (2015); Kumar, Jerbi, Gurrin, and O'Mahony (2014); Terziyski, Albatal, and Gurrin (2015)	The Autographer is a wearable camera that uses sensors widely similar to Microsoft's SenseCam, but is also commercially available
SenseWear (individual data) Kelly and Jones (2009); Sas et al. (2013)	An armband with integrated sensors that allows for the measurement of physiological indicators such as galvanic skin response and skin temperature
Slife (individual data, device-specific data) Kelly and Jones (2009)	"Slife is (. . .) a web service and the Slife client is a very thin application whose sole responsibility is to make desktop activity observations and stream them up to Slife Web."[b]
Smartwatches and further *wearable devices*: (individual data, environment data, device-specific data, third-party data)	
Kelly and Jones (2009)	Polar Heart Rate Monitor
Bao and Choudhury (2010)	iPod Nano (video capture)
Mortazavi et al. (2015)	Samsung Galaxy Gear
Weiss, Timko, Gallagher, Yoneda, and Schreiber (2016)	LG G Watch
Mobile phones (individual data, environment data, device-specific data, third-party data): Nokia (N95, N97): Bao and Choudhury (2010); Ganti, Srinivasan, and Gacic (2010); Kelly and Jones (2009); Miluzzo et al. (2008); Rai, Yan, Chakraborty, Wijaya, and Aberer (2012); Sun, Zhang, and Li (2011); Sun, Zhang, Li, Guo, and Li (2010) Samsung (e.g., Galaxy S2, Galaxy Y, m4650, Galaxy S GT 19000, Nexus S, Galaxy S 4, Galaxy Ace, Galaxy Note II): Anguita, Ghio, Oneto, Parra, and Reyes-Ortiz (2012); Güldenpfennig and Fitzpatrick (2015); Lee and Cho (2013); Mortazavi et al. (2015); Torres-Huitzil and Nuno-Maganda (2015); Weiss et al. (2016)	

[a]The company behind Autographer discontinued operations on 16th October 2016; http://autographer.com/ (04/28/2018)
[b]http://www.slifeweb.com/ (04/28/2018)

Aside from the SenseCam, we highlight other important off-the-shelf devices that have been used in the combined 155 lifelogging studies (see Table 3). As can be seen, not only have wearable cameras and mobile phones been used in previous lifelogging research, but also software to track individual interaction with ICTs (Slife), fitness trackers (e.g., Polar Heart Rate Monitor), smartwatches (e.g., Samsung Galaxy Gear), and dedicated physiological tracking devices such as the SenseWear armband, which can capture skin-related indices that are of importance for stress research (e.g., galvanic skin response, Riedl, Kindermann, Auinger, & Javor, 2013). This overview shows that a wide variety of off-the-shelf devices offers the capabilities (e.g., sensors, processing power, storage) to be applied to continuous data capture.

To overcome some of the specific limitations highlighted in reviewed longitudinal OS studies, we further reviewed a number of additional lifelogging devices. For this purpose, we explored the tool guide of the Quantified Self,[1] an international group of lifelogging enthusiasts, and conducted a keyword-based search for stress-related applications (see Sect. 3 in the chapter "Appendix").

Related to limitations of captured data ("Limited Capture"), multiple of the reviewed OS studies highlighted the need for multi-method designs, pronouncing the potential threat of common method bias due to the exclusive use of self-report measures (e.g., Brennan et al., 2002; Edwards et al., 2007; Finne, Knardahl, & Lau, 2011; Idris, Dollard, & Yulita, 2014; Moen et al., 2013). Particular research that was in need of more objective measures included for example the measurement of individual behaviors such as the performance at work (e.g., Brennan et al., 2002; Finne et al., 2011) or behavior in the social context such as bullying or harassment (e.g., Edwards et al., 2007). For the capture of social interactions, audio tracking can be of use (e.g., mobile phones), but also visual data can be helpful as it allows for the reconstruction of an individual's daily life (e.g., using SenseCam). Regarding performance tracking, device-specific data using applications such as Slife could present an interesting measurement opportunity. In addition, these tools allow for context-independent measurement (e.g., at work, but also at home), which can help to track spillover effects (e.g., positive or negative affect from work spilling over to the private domain, Ilies et al., 2007).

In addition to behaviors and the social interactions, multiple researchers called for a more objective approach to the measurement of health-related data (e.g., Idris et al., 2014; Moen et al., 2013). For this purpose, a multitude of tools that track physiological indicators could be presented here, including the SenseWear armband (heart rate, skin conductance and skin temperature), or, if continuous measurement is not required, mobile apps using the mobile phone's camera for pulse measurement (e.g., Stress Check,[2] Instant Heart Rate[3]).

Regarding the effort related to measurement routines and their potential impact on sample characteristics (e.g., leading to healthy worker effects, Croon, Sluiter, Blonk, Broersen, & Frings-Dresen, 2004; Pas et al., 2012), lifelogging tools can also be of value. For example, most of the devices listed in Table 3 can easily accompany an individual throughout the day and applications such as Slife for performance tracking can capture data in the background of used devices without interference with a participant's activities. Also, due to the low levels of effort required from participants and the context-independent nature of capture with lifelogging tools, researchers could more easily get access to individuals with profound strain (e.g., burned out or otherwise ill individuals, Grau-Alberola, Gil-Monte, Garcia-Juesas, & Figueiredo-Ferraz, 2010; Pas et al., 2012).

---

[1]http://quantifiedself.com/guide/tools/ (04/28/2018).

[2]https://itunes.apple.com/app/stress-check-by-azumio-lite/id500590587?mt=8 (04/28/2018).

[3]http://www.azumio.com/s/instantheartrate/index.html (04/28/2018).

For construct domains which do not allow for objective measurement (i.e., involving subjective experiences, such as perceptions of task difficulty or organizational climate), there are also lifelogging tools, which can at least reduce the effort for individuals to keep diaries of their experiences. For example, GottaFeeling[4] is a mobile app that can be used to log memorable emotional events and the context they happened in, or meQuilibrium[5] is an online platform that can be used to assess sources of stress at work and manually log levels of psychological distress.

Overall, the types of data that can be captured and the off-the-shelf devices that can be used for continuous data collection signify the potential of lifelogging tools and practices for OS research. Yet, the amassed data also has to be analyzed and it has previously been indicated that information retrieval is still a significant challenge in lifelogging research (Gurrin et al., 2014). In the next section we elaborate on prevalent inferences relevant to the six OS construct domains, thereby indicating the maturity of data analysis techniques in each domain.

3.2.2 Information Retrieval

For our classification, we regarded all types of conceptual abstractions as an inference (e.g., the inference of location from GPS coordinates), which was the case in 66 out of the 86 publications in our extended review. We classified which of the six domains of OS-related constructs (input side: task context, social context, physical context; output side: psychological, physiological, behavioral; Fig. 1) can be informed by inferences based on the four types of lifelogging data discussed in the previous section (individual, environment, device-specific, third-party). In Table 4, we present the results of our classification.[6]

Table 4 indicates that we analyzed how often each type of data has been captured. For example, 56 out of 86 publications captured at least one kind of individual data (65%). Also, Table 4 shows absolute and relative frequency of inferences for each construct domain in relation to the overall number of publications (e.g., 15%, 13 out of 86 publications, made an inference relevant to the task context). For each type of data we also indicate how often they were included when inferences about a specific construct domain were made (e.g., 46%, 6 out of 13 publications, used individual data to make an inference relevant to constructs in the task context).

Environmental data, and particularly visual lifelogs, have been most frequently used for inferences on the input side of the stress process, while individual data has most often been used to infer constructs on the output side. Inferences of constructs

[4]https://itunes.apple.com/app/gottafeeling/id393588721?mt=8 (04/28/2018).

[5]https://www.mequilibrium.com/ (04/28/2018).

[6]Coding was done by the first author, the second author independently reviewed the results and there was 100% agreement (note that this result is not surprising because in this classification task there was de facto no room for interpretation). For a list of all 155 publications and the respective classifications please refer to Sect. 2 in the chapter "Appendix".

Table 4 Use of lifelogging data for inferences on OS-related construct domains

		N (%)	Individual	Environment	Device-specific	Third party
	N (%)	86 (–)	56 (65%)	64 (74%)	19 (22%)	6 (7%)
Input (OS)	Task	13 (15%)	6 (46%)	11 (85%)	3 (23%)	1 (8%)
	Social	16 (19%)	7 (44%)	14 (88%)	5 (31%)	1 (6%)
	Physical	30 (35%)	14 (47%)	26 (87%)	4 (13%)	2 (7%)
Output (OS)	Psychological	5 (6%)	2 (40%)	3 (60%)	1 (20%)	0 (–)
	Physiological	54 (63%)	41 (76%)	24 (44%)	3 (6%)	1 (2%)
	Behavioral	60 (70%)	41 (68%)	33 (55%)	7 (12%)	2 (3%)

related to individual cognition (e.g., interest in a stimulus or affective states) are rare in contemporary lifelogging studies (only 6% of reviewed studies, see Table 4). Similarly, direct assessment of physiological indicators is rare too (only two studies in our extended review, as will be highlighted further below).

Input Side

One study assessed whether constructs related to the *task context* can be captured directly through lifelogging tools (i.e., capture of computer-based tasks). Byrne et al. (2008) used the SenseCam to infer individual work activities based on captured images. Due to the low sampling rate (i.e., one picture about every 20–30 s), it was not possible to accurately capture the tasks of knowledge workers from this type of data alone. Twelve studies focused on the inference of everyday activities from lifelogging data, including whether an individual was working or not; also, a more fine-grained distinction of work activities was performed, including giving a presentation, having a professional meeting, typing at the desk, or reading at the desk (Ganti et al., 2010; Jalali & Jain, 2013). The large majority of these studies used visual data or motion data to infer the activities.

In the *social context*, we found four studies which mainly inferred characteristics of the social environment from captured data. Two of them inferred speech (e.g., tracking of conversations) from audio data (Miluzzo et al., 2008; Vemuri, Schmandt, & Bender, 2006), and Smith, O'Hara, and Lewis (2011) inferred the presence of other individuals from faces detected in images as well as from available signals of activated Bluetooth devices (e.g., mobile phones) carried by other individuals. The arguably most intense focus on the social environment was found in a study by Bao and Choudhury (2010), who were most interested in group-level processes. They used accelerometer, compass, audio, and visual data to determine movements and orientation and positive affect was assessed through laughter. Twelve studies also inferred everyday activities from lifelogging data that can be interesting for OS researchers, such as social interactions in the work context, or the occurrence of professional meetings (e.g., Jalali & Jain, 2013; Rai et al., 2012; Wang, Sun, Yang, Smeaton, & Gurrin, 2016).

We found that most studies make inferences relevant for the *physical context*; the dominant inference is to location, which is technically done through GPS coordinates. Another approach in this category uses a mobile phone's Bluetooth for positioning of a person within buildings relative to other static devices with activated Bluetooth (Smith et al., 2011).

Oliver et al. (2013) used visual lifelogging data to infer a number of features of the environment that can be part of a walking or cycling journey. The extracted features included not only objects that could be visible during such a journey (e.g., bus stop, litter, trees), but also information on the weather conditions (e.g., rain) as well as the lighting levels (e.g., visibility of street lighting). Yet, in order to detect these environmental features, sample images were still manually labelled which required significant effort by coders (i.e., in this case, 25 working hours to process about 2300 images equivalent to just more than 6 hours of journey time). Such an approach, if applied to the working environment (e.g., Li, Crane, Gurrin, & Ruskin, 2016; Lim, Lee, & Cho, 2016), can help OS researchers to reconstruct the day of an individual, and particularly to analyze aspects of the physical environment that are potentially stress-inducing (e.g., furniture layout, spatial organization, lighting, tools and equipment applied, as well as architectonical details like colors or decoration used in buildings, Vischer, 2007). As an example, it has been found that room setup in red, if compared to other colors, may significantly activate the sympathetic part of the autonomic nervous system, thereby increasing arousal and stress (e.g., Küller, Mikellides, & Janssens, 2009).

We also found eleven studies that inferred activities from lifelogging data, which took note of aspects of the individual's current physical environment, ranging from some minimal aspects of the environment (e.g., included in physical activities such as going upstairs or downstairs, Wang et al., 2016), to the specific types of places visited by the individual (e.g., home, work, cinema, pub or bar, Wang & Smeaton, 2013).

Output Side

One limitation of lifelogging for the measurement of OS constructs which we have identified based on our review is the paucity of studies (i.e., we identified only five studies in our sample) with a focus on the inference of *psychological outputs* from captured data.

For example, Ohsawa, Takashio, and Tokuda (2006) extracted the level of interaction with applications and data items (e.g., documents, music titles, web pages) to infer the potential interest an individual could have in them. Information on interest, in turn, can potentially foster inferences on personal characteristics (e.g., types of music the individual is interested in, or, in combination with physiological data, which songs can help to relax).

Though only few lifelogging studies focused on psychological outputs explicitly, there are several lifelogging tools that can be helpful to OS researchers. For example, AnalyzeWords[7] (developed at the University of Texas at Austin and the Auckland Medical School in New Zealand) is an online service that can be used to analyze Twitter messages and abstract speech patterns of an individual (e.g., anger or worries indicated by style of writing). Such text analyses can be informative of the psychological state of an individual (e.g., if an individual shows more profound signs of anger or worry during times of high workload).

Also, an additional six studies in our extended review included the measurement of *physiological* indicators. For example, Kelly and Jones (2009) wanted to find out whether the memorability of an event could be inferred from three different physiological indicators of individual arousal (i.e., changes in electro-dermal activity, heart rate, and skin temperature). They found that skin temperature is an unobtrusive indicator of individual arousal levels and can reliably predict the memorability of events without self-reports. Further, Sas et al. (2013) also focused on the measurement of arousal indicators (i.e., electro-dermal activity, measured using Bodymedia's SenseWear device) to assess the potential importance of events captured with the SenseCam.

Still, many studies inferred physical activities from lifelogging data, mainly using motion data or visual data. Such activities (e.g., sitting, standing, walking) can be highly informative for OS research applying physiological measurements, particularly for control purposes (e.g., inferring whether changes in heart rate are actually indicative of cognitive stress processes or whether they have been caused by increased levels of physical activity).

The biggest potential for OS researchers interested in inferences on the output side of the stress process can arguably be found for the *behavioral level*. Aside from the inference of postures or physical activities, "complex activities" inferred from lifelogging data (e.g., eating, shopping, socializing, Jalali & Jain, 2013; Lee & Cho, 2013; Terziyski et al., 2015) can be interesting for OS researchers. As lifelogging is typically faced with the problem of a semantic gap between the facts captured by each single sensor involved and what actually happened from an individual's point of view (Apduhan, Takata, Ma, & Huang, 2008), more meaningful inferences can be derived by combining content (activities) with context (e.g., places or time of day). Fourteen studies conducted such analyses, though surprisingly most of them used only one type of data to infer complex activities, either visual data or motion data, while only three studies used a combination of data types (i.e., accelerometer and audio data, Ganti et al., 2010; environmental and device-specific data, Lee & Cho, 2013; all four types of data, Jalali & Jain, 2013).

Due to the importance of activity recognition in reviewed lifelogging studies and their potential for OS research, we summarized which OS construct domains can be

[7] http://www.analyzewords.com/ (04/28/2018).

Table 5 Relevance of activity recognition for OS construct domains

	Task	Social	Physical	Psychological	Physiological	Behavioral
Information Retrieval (N = 66/86)	13	16	30	5	54	60
Activity Recognition (AR)	13	11	21	1	45	48
Main Sources (AR):						
Visual	9	8	11	1	13	14
Motion	5	6	14	1	36	36

informed by inferred activities and which types of data have been used as basis for these inferences (see Table 5; e.g., 13 out of 13 studies which inferred information relevant for the task context focused on activity recognition, of which nine used visual data and five motion data).

Importantly, most of the reviewed studies which focus on activity recognition adopted or developed automated ways to analyze collected data. Based on features extracted from the captured data sources (e.g., color histogram of images, Terziyski et al., 2015; or number of movements per minute in the case of accelerometer data, Kerr, Marshall, Godbole, Chen, & Legge, 2013), a variety of different activities (up to 23 in our sample of studies, Wang et al., 2016) can be automatically classified by algorithms. Such classifications are also an application of what is commonly referred to as "machine learning" due to more complex algorithms not simply applying a provided rule set (e.g., a simple threshold which determines how many movements per minute indicate walking or sitting), but rather learning schemes to differentiate between activities (e.g., based on previously classified training data) (Preece et al., 2009). An overview of the most popular classification techniques in our sample of reviewed studies as well as exemplary studies which applied them can be found in Table 6.

The prevalence of inferences for each of our six construct domains in the reviewed studies signifies that information retrieval techniques in lifelogging research have become particularly mature for OS-related inputs (i.e., context information, particularly inferred from visual data) and individual behavior on the output side of the stress process (i.e., activity recognition, particularly from visual data or motion data).

3.2.3 Dynamic Aspects

In the OS literature (particularly in the reviewed longitudinal studies), researchers emphasize the difficulty of choosing the right number of measurement points and an adequate lag between them. For example, Nielsen, Randall, and Albertsen (2007) highlight the uncertainty related to the timescale with which different stress effects may become apparent in an organizational context (e.g., effects of work redesign). Rizzuto, Mohammed, and Vance (2011) added that difficulties can already arise

Table 6 Classification techniques used for activity recognition in lifelogging studies

Classification technique	Description (based on Preece et al., 2009)
Decision trees Exemplary Studies: Jalali and Jain (2013); Miluzzo et al. (2008); Wu, Lemaire, and Baddour (2012)	In a decision tree, a set of hierarchically aligned rules (decision nodes) is used for classification. In the context of machine learning, these hierarchies are derived from the extracted features and classifications in a training dataset. The aim for the used algorithm is to create the simplest set of rules that can most likely discriminate between classes
Hidden Markov models Exemplary Studies: Ganti et al. (2010); Lee and Cho (2011); Wang and Smeaton (2013)	In Hidden Markov models, changes in observable states are used for classification purposes. These observable changes are with a certain likelihood related to changes in some hidden states, which are of actual interest. These hidden states and the changes from one to another are expected to have a constant likelihood and may cause one or more of the changes in observable states. For example, changes in posture (observable via accelerometer) can be informative of individual movement (hidden), such as sitting not being likely after ascending stairs, hence offering information on how to discriminate between physical activities based on changes in posture
Support vector machines Exemplary Studies: Anguita et al. (2012); Rai et al. (2012); Sun et al. (2010, 2011); Terziyski et al. (2015)	Based on training data with known classifications of objects, support vector machines aim to find a path between classes that allows for optimum discrimination (i.e., highest margin between classes of objects). Importantly, this path is not limited to a linear function, but can also be non-linear if additional dimensions are added to the vector space that data objects are projected into (i.e., using kernel functions) instead of a simple path (original space), the algorithm then has to find a hyperplane (higher-dimensional space) that separates classes from each other
Further techniques	Artificial neural networks (Khan, Siddiqi, & Lee, 2013), Bayesian networks (Lee & Cho, 2013), Conditional random field (Wang et al., 2016), Hierarchical neural classifier (Torres-Huitzil & Nuno-Maganda, 2015), and Mixture-of-experts model (Lee & Cho, 2014)

from the conceptual definition of effects. As an example from the information systems implementation domain: When does an implementation period start and end, and when do implemented changes take effect?

In this context, we highlight that only two points of measurement, which have most often been used in the reviewed studies (see Sect. 2 in chapter "Appendix"), lead to limitations for data analysis. For example, two points of measurement are not enough to detect potential mediating effects, which would require at least three measurement points with each variable of interest being measured at each point of data collection (e.g., Petrou et al., 2015; Reknes et al., 2014).

Importantly, as we live in a spatiotemporal world (i.e., at all times we are, physically, at one location), most of the inferences presented in the last section also inherently focus on the dynamic aspects of our life. In other words, the nature of lifelogging implies that data are captured in a longitudinal fashion. Hence, lifelogging seems well suited to overcome well-known methodological limitations in the OS research literature.

In addition to calling for more frequent measurements, several OS studies have also called for shorter time spans between measurements and Bono et al. (2013) even proposed that 24-h monitoring might be a fruitful avenue to understand the links between specific stressors, strains and individual health as indicated by physiological measures.

For the analysis of the resulting, highly granular data, most lifelogging studies which we reviewed first applied a segmentation of continuous streams of data into discrete *events* (e.g., Cho et al., 2007; Hwang & Cho, 2009; Kumar et al., 2014). This routine, among others, mimics how individuals memorize their everyday life. One common approach in this context is the event segmentation process introduced by Doherty and Smeaton (2008). Confronted with the vast number of images that can be collected over the course of a day using the SenseCam (i.e., about 3000 images), they used visual features of images to determine their similarity, or a level of change, that would signify a different event (e.g., change in context or activities). Monroe (2008) pointed out that measurement via events is still amongst the most prominent practices in stress research which are applied in order to identify sources of life stress across individuals.

However, event-based analysis of lifelogging data may not be granular enough to detect the many daily *hassles* with which we are confronted in the work environment and which may disturb our work routine (e.g., unusually long response times of information systems or unexpected interruptions by colleagues). Such more detailed analyses require a high level of temporal granularity and, though widely prevalent in lifelogging studies, visual data may not be suitable to satisfy data requirements due to the low sampling rates of wearable camera devices (e.g., as shown for the capture of computer-related tasks by Byrne et al., 2008). While the SenseCam only achieves a sampling rate of about 1/20 to 1/30 Hz (i.e., one image about every 20–30 s), other popular types of lifelogging data could help to overcome this weakness.[8] For example, while most of the studies which applied an accelerometer to capture individual motion used a sampling rate of about 10 Hz, none went below 5 Hz (e.g., Gurrin, Qiu, et al., 2013; Zhang, McCullagh, Zhang, & Yu, 2014), due to, among other reasons, power consumption (i.e., lower sampling rates enable longer durations of measurement). Nonetheless, higher sampling rates are technically

[8]The unit of signal frequency used is Hertz (Hz). The Hz is equivalent to cycles per second. Hz is named after Heinrich R. Hertz (1857–1894), a German physicist who first conclusively proved the existence of electromagnetic waves.

possible even on off-the-shelf devices (e.g., 100 Hz on smartphones and smartwatches, Mortazavi et al., 2015), though none of the reviewed studies actually used such a high sampling rate in a longitudinal field study. Yet, the by far highest granularity amongst the more common data sources in lifelogging studies can be found for audio data, with a sampling rate of 8 kHz (8000 data points per second) being commonly used (e.g., Blum et al., 2006; Ganti et al., 2010).

What is the implication of this discussion for OS stress research? One solution is the combination of data sources in order to detect more temporally granular aspects relevant to OS. For example, while visual data can help to get a good idea of the content of daily events and their main context (e.g., working in the office), additional data streams can be used to get in-depth knowledge of events (e.g., physical activities inferred from accelerometer data for jobs that involve a significant number of physically-demanding tasks or speech and conversations inferred from audio data for the capture of social interactions which might be potentially stressful). Such an approach has, for example, been presented by Smith et al. (2011) who also emphasized the inference limitation related to the use of one data source alone (i.e., location from GPS). Therefore, they added further data sources (i.e., images, Bluetooth detection). The combination of data sources allowed, for example, the inference of individual tendencies to take breaks (i.e., changing location and being in the vicinity of the same co-workers), which can be valuable for OS researchers who are interested in the stress coping strategies of individuals, among other topics.

In addition to calling for higher granularity of captured data (i.e., more frequent measurement), researchers have also made a call for longer periods of measurement. For example, Hyvonen et al. (2011) suggested that measurement over longer periods of time can help us to understand changes in the work context or the development of individual work-related goals. Because proper understanding of individual goals is fundamental for insight into the development of human stress processes (Cummings & Cooper, 1979; Edwards, 1992), complementary inference of goals based on lifelogging data (in addition to self-reported data) may be valuable to OS researchers.

Analyses of lifelogging data on the level of events or even hassles can then be used to inform *longitudinal* stress development patterns. For example, Doherty et al. (2011) derived behavioral patterns (i.e., lifestyle) from visual lifelogging data. Participants consisted of four main groups (i.e., regular lifeloggers, office workers, researchers, retirees) who wore the SenseCam for a period of up to 3.5 years. Concepts were extracted from the users' visual lifelogs and it was possible to infer certain lifestyle traits of individual groups. For example, office workers used their lunch break to eat, while researchers and lifeloggers ate on an irregular basis. Because evidence (Boucsein & Thum, 1997) indicates that design of work breaks affects recovery from stress, work break data (collected through lifelogging) helps to better understand stress processes.

Further studies analyzed the periodicities of events and how they cluster over time. For example, Abe et al. (2009) and Huang et al. (2015) analyzed the travel behavior of individuals and derived journey patterns and the places individuals visited regularly. For OS research, such patterns could be interesting, particularly if we focus on irregularities. For example, bad mood can be caused by work-related stressors (Vrijkotte, van Doornen, & de Geus, 2000), but could also be an effect of stressors unrelated to an individual's work, such as irregularities in the daily commute to the office (e.g., traffic jam). The inference of such an additional cause of stress would hardly be possible without lifelogging data. As another example, through longitudinal location tracking (e.g., using Where Have I Been,[9] a mobile app for location tracking) it is possible to assess the normal route and regular time it takes for an individual to commute to work. Such data could confirm that a possible delay has actually been caused by a traffic jam and not some other circumstance (e.g., the car broke down); traffic data is an example of third-party data in lifelogging research.

For OS research interested in the chronic effects of stress, our review of longitudinal studies indicates that several years of data collection are feasible, with the largest lag between measurement points having been applied by Tyson and Pongruengphant (2004), with 5 years between both points. As lifelogging is still a young discipline with life-encompassing self-tracking only being possible for about 15 years (e.g., MyLifeBits, formerly "CyberAll", see Bell, 2001), such longitudinal examples of lifelogging are still rare.

For example, in our review of lifelogging studies, we only found 15 papers (including the self-tracking activities by Gordon Bell, Gemmell et al., 2006) which used more than a year's worth of data (in some cases captured non-consecutively) for their analyses (e.g., up to 4 years of data: Isaacs et al., 2013; 5 years: Huang et al., 2015; 10 years: Hu, Smeaton, & Newman, 2014). Still, it has been emphasized, for example by Mitchell and James (2001), that analyses which build on the time dimension benefit from such longitudinal datasets, and particularly "[f]or various analysis issues, more people and more occasions are usually better. They (...) provide us with more confidence in our inferences." (p. 538).

4 Discussion, Limitations, and Future Research

Based on the review of lifelogging literature and the informational needs in OS research, we can highlight a number of areas that still require additional research in order to further increase the value of lifelogging for OS research.

On the *input side* of the stress process we see particular potential for OS research regarding the tracking of overall work patterns (e.g., number of hours worked per week or overall work-life balance). However, our review also reveals that detailed inferences that we would have expected before the analysis of the lifelogging studies (e.g., progress made on projects throughout a work day inferred from device-specific data) have not yet been reported in the literature (but are technologically feasible).

Importantly, lifelogging data can be used to reliably capture details of individual interactions (e.g., including speech recognition), which could inform researchers of potential stressors (e.g., interpersonal conflicts) or the general relationship with other

[9] https://itunes.apple.com/us/app/journey-journal-that-writes/id641553983?mt=8 (04/28/2018).

individuals at work (e.g., level of interaction with colleagues and supervisors, potential sources of social support), particularly if combined with inferences on individual outputs (e.g., psychophysiological indicators of arousal). Yet, more subtle constructs on a higher level of analysis (e.g., organizational climate or cultural norms) have not received as much attention in the reviewed studies, with the main exception being the study by Bao and Choudhury (2010), who focused on the group level.

Regarding the physical context, we were surprised that the types of data that could potentially be informative of the physical environment were not involved in any analyses. For example, device-specific data which can inform the status of work-related equipment, or environmental sensors integrated in the SenseCam providing information on light levels and ambient temperatures, have not been used in contemporary lifelogging research. Yet, this fact does not diminish their potential value for OS research.

On the *output side*, there is a paucity of studies directly applicable to the measurement of psychological outputs relevant to the OS process (e.g., signs of depression, commitment, coping efforts, or physiological states in general). Currently, there is more of a focus on the creation of an external memory which can then be the basis for information retrieval. Some lifelogging applications still include manual annotations by individuals (e.g., textual or vocal comments), thereby providing researchers with information on individual appraisal of given situations (e.g., Güldenpfennig & Fitzpatrick, 2015; Huang et al., 2015). Hence, based on current lifelogging technology, there is still a need for self-reports to develop insight into psychological constructs which are relevant to OS research.

Also, only few studies in our reviewed sample used devices, such as fitness trackers (e.g., Hu et al., 2014; Jalali & Jain, 2013; Sas et al., 2013), that could be applied to unobtrusively capture physiological indicators, hence limiting the current potential of lifelogging practices for OS research in this regard. However, lifelogging researchers (e.g., Dobbins & Fairclough, 2015) have previously highlighted that physiological data in combination with contextual information can be highly informative of how certain situations in our daily lives make us feel. Hence, potential developments in this domain are to be expected in the near future. In this context, the concept of diagnosticity is pivotal. Diagnosticity is "a property of a measure, and describes how precisely it captures a target construct as opposed to other constructs" (Riedl, Davis, & Hevner, 2014, p. xviii). It follows that if a physiological measure represents only one construct in the OS process, but not other constructs, its diagnosticity is maximal. However, a perfect one-to-one relationship between physiological measures and psychological constructs does not exist (Cacioppo & Tassinary, 1990). Rather, one physiological measure (e.g., arousal measured via skin conductance) is often related to multiple constructs (e.g., interest, negative affect, pleasure; see Riedl et al., 2014). Thus, 100% diagnosticity is theoretically possible, but it is very unlikely that it can ever be established in reality in psychophysiological research, particularly in a complex research domain such as OS. Researchers should therefore strive for a high degree of diagnosticity, while accepting that it can never be fully reached.

There is a *large number of more recent devices* for the capture of data related to each of our construct domains that could be applied to OS research and should be tested in this regard. For example, popular fitness tracking devices such as the ones provided by FitBit[10] could be applied to the tracking of physiological indicators (e.g., the FitBit Surge wristband to track cardiovascular data), or more exotic devices such as the Emvio watch[11] measuring heart rate variability for continuous stress management, or biometric clothing provided by Hexoskin.[12] Also, there is a plethora of software applications that could be interesting for OS researchers, such as RescueTime[13] as an alternative to Slife for time tracking, Menthal,[14] a mobile app for the tracking of mobile phone usage, and Tracktackular[15] for the management of a variety of tracked data, just to list a selection of examples.[16]

A particular *limitation* of the applicability of more recent lifelogging tools to OS research is the need to first check reliability and validity of measurement. For example, energy expenditure that can be inferred from physical activities has been the focus of Lee, Kim, and Welk (2014) who compared a number of fitness trackers (e.g., Nike+ Fuelband and FitBit One) with the SenseWear armband. They found that while the SenseWear's estimations of energy expenditure resulted in an error of 8–9% compared to a gold standard, the rest of the monitors yielded discrepancies from actual energy expenditure of 10–15% and even beyond. Yet, more recently, Tucker, Bhammar, Sawyer, Buman, and Gaesser (2015) found that a common fitness tracker (i.e., Nike+ Fuelband) can provide estimations of energy expenditure that are comparable to the Sensewear's estimations, though it is a device that is more specialized for physiological tracking. Hence, while it can be assumed that the collection of raw data is not much of an issue in most cases (e.g., technology use being tracked by installed software), the inferences from these types of data that are often also provided should be used with caution. Ideally, only devices for which validation studies have been conducted and published should be used, which is easy to assess in some domains (e.g., in the case of self-measurement devices for blood pressure[17]).

Further, many confounding factors have to be considered when applying non-clinical devices to OS research, such as the actual placement of the sensors (e.g., mobile phones being carried in trouser pockets, wristbands, armbands, neck-worn devices, head-mounted devices). For example, Taraldsen et al. (2011) reported

[10]https://www.fitbit.com/ (04/28/2018).

[11]http://emvio.watch/ (04/28/2018).

[12]http://www.hexoskin.com/ (04/28/2018).

[13]https://www.rescuetime.com/ (04/28/2018).

[14]https://play.google.com/store/apps/details?id=open.menthal&hl=eng (04/28/2018).

[15]https://www.tracktacular.com/ (04/28/2018).

[16]Discussions on further lifelogging tools and related field reports can be found at: https://forum.quantifiedself.com/c/quantified-self/apps-tools (04/28/2018).

[17]http://www.dableducational.org/sphygmomanometers/devices_2_sbpm.html#AUTOMATED_SPHYGMOMANOMETERS_FOR_SELFMEASUREMENT (04/28/2018).

that step counts gathered with an accelerometer were affected by the placement of the sensor on patients with hip fractures, leading to an underestimation of step counts if placed on an impaired limb. In another exemplary study, Wolf, Schmidt, Bexheti, and Langheinrich (2014) compared devices that can be used to create a visual lifelog. They demonstrated that form factor and positioning of wearable cameras (e.g., integrated into glasses, worn on neck-level or on chest-level) resulted in significantly different representations of the environment, in some cases hardly comparable regarding the types of concepts that were captured.

In addition, the limitations of this review, mainly focusing on the technological capabilities of lifelogging tools and practices, have to be kept in mind. Particularly socio-ethical concerns that are related to the continuous capture of an individual's daily experiences are important when considering the application of lifelogging tools to OS research. Here, we refer to Jacquemard et al. (2014) who reviewed previous lifelogging studies, summarizing those topics that have most often been highlighted as socio-ethical challenges of lifelogging. They found that privacy issues have been by far the most discussed (26 out of 52 reviewed papers), followed by related topics such as the existing legal uncertainties regarding the ownership of lifelogging data or its retention after the death of the lifelogger. Dodge and Kitchin (2007) further noted the importance of data privacy in the organizational context, stating that in the past, forms of individual tracking have often been abused to monitor individuals and present them with behavior-related rewards or punishments. It has to be noted though that such difficulties are not new or exclusive to the lifelogging domain. As Czerwinski et al. (2006) stated, qualitatively there is no visible difference between the privacy concerns related to lifelogging and other domains which handle digital content. Yet, the quantity of data captured and retained might be what makes "a scary situation scarier" (p. 47).

5 Conclusion

We discussed the potential of lifelogging for OS research, particularly regarding the capture of data, inferences on relevant constructs, and time-related analyses to take into account the dynamic aspects of stress. Based on a review of landmark publications and state-of-the-art lifelogging research and technology, we can draw a number of important conclusions pertaining to each of these three domains and the methodological limitations related to them.

First, regarding the capture of data, we can emphasize the high potential of off-the-shelf consumer-grade devices for research in field settings, such as OS. Already frequently discussed in the reviewed publications, mobile phones (i.e., smartphones) are the most important tool for researchers who want to add individual self-tracking to their repertoire of data collection methods. Also, new types of devices designed for consumer-level applications already reach the level of capabilities of mobile phones for some applications (e.g., smartwatches instead of smartphones to track activities which involve frequent hand movements, Weiss et al., 2016). Hence, both smartphones and smartwatches are viable measurement devices for OS researchers (assuming that the devices' reliability and validity have been established).

Second, visual data is among the most frequently captured types of data in lifelogging research and among the most useful for OS research. In the studies we reviewed, most contextual information had been derived from continuous visual lifelogs, and also latent variables, such as interestingness of a stimulus, have often been inferred based on this type of data. Still, as we have highlighted for each of our six domains, there can be other types of data that can satisfy more specific information needs. For example, audio data has been shown to be a valuable source if a researcher is interested in the social context of an individual, and we have argued that device-specific data is of potential interest for inferences on constructs in the task context (e.g., interruptions by notifications or general switching behavior indicating disruptive factors for task performance). Further, the tracking of individual behavior has been shown to be a main application of lifelogging which is of high value to OS. In essence, instead of cost and time-intensive field observations, and as a complementary data source to self-reports, which are prone to social desirability bias and memory distortion, OS researchers could use individual behavior tracking devices and/or devices that capture physiological states of individuals.

Third, lifelogging typically provides highly granular data on a longitudinal basis. Most people carry their mobile phones with them throughout the day, or at least have them in their vicinity. Hence, unobtrusive measurement using such constantly available devices without any further effort by their owner is achievable and particularly valuable for OS research, as captured data is not limited to one situation, but reflects most of an individual's daily life, typically both at work and at home.

Against the background of the results of our review, we emphasize the value of lifelogging for OS research and particularly longitudinal studies in the field. Overall, we found the greatest potential for OS research in the domain of behavioral outputs. For example, we can infer, at least to some degree, an individual's nutrient balance from lifelogging data based on eating behaviors (e.g., Aizawa, Maruyama, Li, & Morikawa, 2013; Jalali & Jain, 2013; Weiss et al., 2016) and dietary choices (e.g., visual data, Aizawa et al., 2013). This, in turn, can potentially provide information on the impact of stress on health behaviors and the way in which individuals cope with acute stress (e.g., unhealthy eating behaviors). Also, we can derive other behaviors that individuals choose to cope with stress from lifelogging data such as taking breaks (e.g., by identifying sedentary behaviors from accelerometer data, Rai et al., 2012), exercising (e.g., from accelerometer data, Weiss et al., 2016; or environmental and device-specific data, Lee & Cho, 2013), or spending time with others (e.g., from visual data, Terziyski et al., 2015).

In conclusion, we can state that methods and tools applied in lifelogging can be a valuable addition to OS research, particularly for longitudinal investigations in field settings. Like all measurement approaches those from the lifelogging domain also have strengths and weaknesses. Therefore, lifelogging constitutes a complement to the more traditional measurement approaches in OS research (e.g., survey, interview, hormone assessment), and not a substitute. It will be rewarding to see what insight future OS research based on lifelogging methods and tools reveals.

Acknowledgements This research was funded by the Upper Austrian Government as part of the PhD program "Digital Business International", a joint initiative between the University of Applied Sciences Upper Austria and the University of Linz, and as part of the project "Digitaler Stress in Unternehmen" (Basisfinanzierungsprojekt) at the University of Applied Sciences Upper Austria.

References

Abe, M., Morinishi, Y., Maeda, A., Aoki, M., & Inagaki, H. (2009). A life log collector integrated with a remote-controller for enabling user centric services. *IEEE Transactions on Consumer Electronics, 55*(1), 295–302. https://doi.org/10.1109/TCE.2009.4814448

Aizawa, K., Maruyama, Y., Li, H., & Morikawa, C. (2013). Food balance estimation by using personal dietary tendencies in a multimedia food log. *IEEE Transactions on Multimedia, 15*(8), 2176–2185. https://doi.org/10.1109/TMM.2013.2271474

Amiot, C. E., Terry, D. J., Jimmieson, N. L., & Callan, V. J. (2006). A longitudinal investigation of coping processes during a merger: Implications for job satisfaction and organizational identification. *Journal of Management, 32*(4), 552–574. https://doi.org/10.1177/0149206306287542

Anderson, N. B., Belar, C. D., Breckler, S. J., Nordal, K. C., Ballard, D. W., Bufka, L. F., ... Rieder, S. (2015). Stress in America: Paying with our health.

Anguita, D., Ghio A., Oneto L., Parra X., & Reyes-Ortiz J. L. (2012). Human activity recognition on smartphones for mobile context awareness. In *Proceedings of the 26th conference on advances in neural information processing systems* (pp. 1–9).

Apduhan, B. O., Takata, K., Ma, J., & Huang, R. (2008). Activity situation model and application prototype for lifelog image analysis. *International Journal of Software Engineering and Its Applications, 2*(4), 31–42.

Bachorowski, J.-A., & Owren, M. J. (1995). Vocal expression of emotion: Acoustic properties of speech are associated with emotional intensity and context. *Psychological Science, 6*(4), 219–224. https://doi.org/10.1111/j.1467-9280.1995.tb00596.x

Bao, X., & Choudhury R. R. (2010). MoVi: Mobile phone based video highlights via collaborative sensing. In S. Banerjee, S. Keshav, & A. Wolman (Eds.), *Proceedings of the 8th international conference on mobile systems, applications, and services (MobiSys 2010)* (pp. 357–370). https://doi.org/10.1145/1814433.1814468

Barley, S. R., Meyerson, D. E., & Grodal, S. (2011). E-mail as a source and symbol of stress. *Organization Science, 22*(4), 887–906. https://doi.org/10.1287/orsc.1100.0573

Beehr, T. A., & Newman, J. E. (1978). Job stress, employee health, and organizational effectiveness: A facet analysis, model, and literature review. *Personnel Psychology, 31*, 665–699. https://doi.org/10.1111/j.1744-6570.1978.tb02118.x

Bell, C. G., & Gemmell, J. (2009). *Total recall: How the e-memory revolution will change everything*. New York: Dutton.

Bell, G. (2001). A personal digital store. *Communications of the ACM, 44*(1), 86–91. https://doi.org/10.1145/357489.357513

Bell, G., & Gemmell, J. (2007). A digital life. *Scientific American, 296*, 58–65.

Biggs, A., Brough, P., & Barbour, J. P. (2014). Relationships of individual and organizational support with engagement: Examining various types of causality in a three-wave study. *Work and Stress, 28*(3), 236–254. https://doi.org/10.1080/02678373.2014.934316

Blum, M., Pentland, A., & Troster, G. (2006). InSense: Interest-based life logging. *IEEE Multimedia, 13*(4), 40–48. https://doi.org/10.1109/MMUL.2006.87

Boell, S. K., & Cecez-Kecmanovic, D. (2014). A hermeneutic approach for conducting literature reviews and literature searches. *Communications of the Association for Information Systems, 34* (1), 12.

Bono, J. E., Glomb, T. M., Shen, W., Kim, E., & Koch, A. J. (2013). Building positive resources: Effects of positive events and positive reflection on work stress and health. *Academy of Management Journal, 56*(6), 1601–1627. https://doi.org/10.5465/amj.2011.0272

Boucsein, W., & Thum, M. (1997). Design of work/rest schedules for computer work based on psychophysiological recovery measures. *International Journal of Industrial Ergonomics, 20*, 51–57. https://doi.org/10.1016/S0169-8141(96)00031-5

Bragard, I., Etienne, A.-M., Merckaert, I., Libert, Y., & Razavi, D. (2010). Efficacy of a communication and stress management training on medical residents' self-efficacy, stress to communicate and burnout A randomized controlled study. *Journal of Health Psychology, 15*(7), 1075–1081. https://doi.org/10.1177/1359105310361992

Brennan, A., Chugh, J. S., & Kline, T. (2002). Traditional versus open office design: A longitudinal field study. *Environment and Behavior, 34*(3), 279–299. https://doi.org/10.1177/0013916502034003001

Brindley, R., Bateman, A., & Gracey, F. (2011). Exploration of use of SenseCam to support autobiographical memory retrieval within a cognitive-behavioural therapeutic intervention following acquired brain injury. *Memory, 19*(7), 745–757. https://doi.org/10.1080/09658211.2010.493893

Bush, V. (1945). As we may think. *The Atlantic Monthly* (July), 112–124.

Byrne, D., Doherty, A. R., Jones, G. J. F., Smeaton, A. F., Kumpulainen, S., & Järvelin, K. (2008). The SenseCam as a tool for task observation. In: O. Abuelmaatti (Ed.), *Proceedings of the 22nd British HCI Group annual conference on people and computers: Culture, creativity, interaction* (pp. 19–22). Swinton: British Computer Society. https://doi.org/10.1145/1531826.1531832

Byrne, D., Doherty, A. R., Snoek, C. G. M., Jones, G. J. F., & Smeaton, A. F. (2010). Everyday concept detection in visual lifelogs: Validation, relationships and trends. *Multimedia Tools and Applications, 49*(1), 119–144. https://doi.org/10.1007/s11042-009-0403-8

Cacioppo, J. T., & Tassinary, L. G. (1990). Inferring psychological significance from physiolgical signals. *American Psychologist, 45*(1), 16–28. https://doi.org/10.1037/0003-066X.45.1.16

California Institute for Telecommunications and Information Technology. (2014). *Personal data for the public good: New opportunities to enrich understanding of individual and population health*. Final report of the health data exploration project.

Carayon, P., Smith, M. J., & Haims, M. C. (1999). Work organization, job stress, and work-related musculoskeletal disorders. *Human Factors: The Journal of the Human Factors and Ergonomics Society, 41*(4), 644–663. https://doi.org/10.1518/001872099779656743

Cavanaugh, M. A., Boswell, W. R., Roehling, M. V., & Boudreau, J. W. (2000). An empirical examination of self-reported work stress among U.S. managers. *Journal of Applied Psychology, 85*(1), 65–74. https://doi.org/10.1037/0021-9010.85.1.65

Childs, J. H., & Stoeber, J. (2012). Do you want me to be perfect? Two longitudinal studies on socially prescribed perfectionism, stress and burnout in the workplace. *Work and Stress, 26*(4), 347–364. https://doi.org/10.1080/02678373.2012.737547

Cho, S.-B., Kim, K. J., Hwang, K. S., & Song, I.-J. (2007). AniDiary: Daily cartoon-style diary exploits Bayesian networks. *IEEE Pervasive Computing, 6*(3), 66–75. https://doi.org/10.1109/MPRV.2007.49

Cooper, C. L., & Cartwright, S. (1994). Healthy mind; Healthy organization—A proactive approach to occupational stress. *Human Relations, 47*(4), 455–471. https://doi.org/10.1177/001872679404700405

Croon, E. M. de, Sluiter, J. K., Blonk, R. W., Broersen, J. P., & Frings-Dresen, M. H. (2004). Stressful work, psychological job strain, and turnover: A 2-year prospective cohort study of truck drivers. *Journal of Applied Psychology, 89*(3), 442–454. https://doi.org/10.1037/0021-9010.89.3.442

Cummings, T. G., & Cooper, C. L. (1979). A cybernetic framework for studying occupational stress. *Human Relations, 32*(5), 395–418. https://doi.org/10.1177/001872677903200504

Czerwinski, M., Gage, D. W., Gemmell, J., Marshall, C. C., Pérez-Quiñones, M. A., Skeels, M. M., & Catarci, T. (2006). Digital memories in an era of ubiquitous computing and abundant storage. *Communications of the ACM, 49*(1), 44. https://doi.org/10.1145/1107458.1107489

Danna, K., & Griffin, R. W. (1999). Health and well-being in the workplace: A review and synthesis of the literature. *Journal of Management, 25*(3), 357–384. https://doi.org/10.1016/S0149-2063(99)00006-9

Dey, A. K. (2001). Understanding and using context. *Personal and Ubiquitous Computing, 5*(1), 4–7. https://doi.org/10.1007/s007790170019

Dobbins, C., & Fairclough, S. (2015). Lifelogging technologies to detect negative emotions associated with cardiovascular disease. In: D. Al-Jumeily, A. Hussain, C. Mallucci, & C. Oliver (Eds.), *Applied computing in medicine and health* (pp. 27–44). Elsevier. https://doi.org/10.1016/B978-0-12-803468-2.00002-3

Dodge, M., & Kitchin, R. (2007). 'Outlines of a world coming into existence': Pervasive computing and the ethics of forgetting. *Environment and Planning B: Planning and Design, 34*(3), 431–445. https://doi.org/10.1068/b32041t

Doherty, A. R., Caprani, N., Conaire, C. Ó., Kalnikaite, V., Gurrin, C., Smeaton, A. F., & O'Connor, N. E. (2011). Passively recognising human activities through lifelogging. *Computers in Human Behavior, 27*(5), 1948–1958. https://doi.org/10.1016/j.chb.2011.05.002

Doherty, A. R., & Smeaton, A. F. (2008). Automatically segmenting lifelog data into events. In IEEE (Ed.), *Proceedings of the ninth international workshop on image analysis for multimedia interactive services* (pp. 20–23). https://doi.org/10.1109/WIAMIS.2008.32

Doherty, A. R., & Smeaton, A. F. (2010). Automatically augmenting lifelog events using pervasively generated content from millions of people. *Sensors, 10*(3), 1423–1446. https://doi.org/10.3390/s100301423

Edwards, J. R. (1992). A cybernetic theory of stress, coping and well-being in organizations. *The Academy of Management Review, 17*(2), 238–274. https://doi.org/10.5465/AMR.1992.4279536

Edwards, J. R., & Bagozzi, R. P. (2000). On the nature and direction of relationships between constructs and measures. *Psychological Methods, 5*(2), 155–174. https://doi.org/10.1037/1082-989X.5.2.155

Edwards, J. A., Guppy, A., & Cockerton, T. (2007). A longitudinal study exploring the relationships between occupational stressors, non-work stressors, and work performance. *Work and Stress, 21*(2), 99–116. https://doi.org/10.1080/02678370701466900

Emurian, H. H. (1993). Cardiovascular and electromyograph effects of low and high density work on an interactive information system. *Computers in Human Behavior, 9*(4), 353–370. https://doi.org/10.1016/0747-5632(93)90028-Q

Evans, G. W., & Johnson, D. (2000). Stress and open-office noise. *Journal of Applied Psychology, 85*(5), 779–783. https://doi.org/10.1037/0021-9010.85.5.779

Finne, L. B., Knardahl, S., & Lau, B. (2011). Workplace bullying and mental distress: A prospective study of Norwegian employees. *Scandinavian Journal of Work Environment and Health, 37*(4), 276–287. https://doi.org/10.5271/sjweh.3156

Fox, S., & Duggan, M. (2013). *Tracking for Health*. Washington, DC: PewResearchCenter.

Frese, M. (1985). Stress at work and psychosomatic complaints: A causal interpretation. *Journal of Applied Psychology, 70*(2), 314–328. https://doi.org/10.1037/0021-9010.70.2.314

Frese, M., & Zapf, D. (1988). Methodological issues in the study of work stress: Objective vs subjective measurement of work stress and the question of longitudinal studies. In C. L. Cooper (Ed.), *Causes, coping and consequences of stress at work* (pp. 375–411). Chichester: Wiley.

Ganti, R. K., Srinivasan, S., & Gacic, A. (2010). Multisensor fusion in smartphones for lifestyle monitoring. In *Proceedings of the 2010 international conference on body sensor networks (BSN)* (pp. 36–43). https://doi.org/10.1109/BSN.2010.10

Gartner. (2015). Gartner says worldwide device shipments to grow 1.5 percent, to reach 2.5 billion units in 2015. Retrieved from http://www.gartner.com/newsroom/id/3088221

Gemmell, J., Bell, G., & Lueder, R. (2006). MyLifeBits: A personal database for everything. *Communications of the ACM, 49*(1), 88–95. https://doi.org/10.1145/1107458.1107460

Goh, J., Pfeffer, J., & Zenios, S. A. (2015). The relationship between workplace stressors and mortality and health costs in the United States. *Management Science, 62*(2), 608–628. https://doi.org/10.1287/mnsc.2014.2115

Grau-Alberola, E., Gil-Monte, P. R., Garcia-Juesas, A. J., & Figueiredo-Ferraz, H. (2010). Incidence of burnout in Spanish nursing professionals: A longitudinal study. *International Journal of Nursing Studies, 47*(8), 1013–1020. https://doi.org/10.1016/j.ijnurstu.2009.12.022

Güldenpfennig, F., & Fitzpatrick, G. (2015). Personal digital archives on mobile phones with MEO. *Personal and Ubiquitous Computing, 19*(2), 445–461. https://doi.org/10.1007/s00779-014-0802-3

Gurrin, C., Qiu, Z., Hughes, M., Caprani, N., Doherty, A. R., Hodges, S. E., & Smeaton, A. F. (2013). The smartphone as a platform for wearable cameras in health research. *American Journal of Preventive Medicine, 44*(3), 308–313. https://doi.org/10.1016/j.amepre.2012.11.010

Gurrin, C., Smeaton, A. F., & Doherty, A. R. (2014). Lifelogging: Personal big data. *Foundations and Trends® in information retrieval, 8*(1), 1–125. https://doi.org/10.1561/1500000033

Gurrin, C., Smeaton, A. F., Qiu, Z., & Doherty, A. R. (2013). Exploring the technical challenges of large-scale lifelogging. In J. Kerr, N. Weibel, & C. Gurrin (Eds.), *Proceedings of the 4th international SenseCam & pervasive imaging conference* (pp. 68–75). https://doi.org/10.1145/2526667.2526678

Hansen, J. H. (1996). Analysis and compensation of speech under stress and noise for environmental robustness in speech recognition. *Speech Communication, 20*(1–2), 151–173. https://doi.org/10.1016/S0167-6393(96)00050-7

Hodges, S., Berry, E., & Wood, K. (2011). SenseCam: A wearable camera that stimulates and rehabilitates autobiographical memory. *Memory, 19*(7), 685–696. https://doi.org/10.1080/09658211.2011.605591

Hu, F., Smeaton, A. F., & Newman, E. (2014). Periodicity detection in lifelog data with missing and irregularly sampled data. In IEEE (Ed.), *Proceedings of BIBM 2014* (pp. 16–23). https://doi.org/10.1109/BIBM.2014.6999284

Huang, F.-M., Huang, Y. H., Szu, C., Su, A. Y., Chen, M. C., & Sun, Y. S. (2015). A study of a life logging smartphone app and its power consumption observation in location-based service scenario. In *Proceedings of the 2015 I.E. international conference on mobile services (MS)* (pp. 225–232). https://doi.org/10.1109/MobServ.2015.40

Hwang, K.-S., & Cho, S.-B. (2009). Landmark detection from mobile life log using a modular bayesian network model. *Expert Systems with Applications, 36*(10), 12065–12076. https://doi.org/10.1016/j.eswa.2009.03.002

Hyvonen, K., Feldt, T., Kinnunen, U., & Tolvanen, A. (2011). Changes in personal work goals in relation to the psychosocial work environment: A two-year follow-up study. *Work and Stress, 25*(4), 289–308. https://doi.org/10.1080/02678373.2012.630587

Idris, M. A., Dollard, M. F., & Yulita. (2014). Psychosocial safety climate, emotional demands, burnout, and depression: A longitudinal multilevel study in the Malaysian private sector. *Journal of Occupational Health Psychology, 19*(3), 291–302. https://doi.org/10.1037/a0036599

Idris, M. K., O'Driscoll, M. P., & Anderson, M. H. (2011). Longitudinal mediation effects of strain on the relationships between role stressors and employees' withdrawal responses. *Stress and Health, 27*(5), 403–412. https://doi.org/10.1002/smi.1392

Ilies, R., Schwind, K. M., Wagner, D. T., & Johnson, M. D. (2007). When can employees have a family life ? the effects of daily workload and affect on work-family conflict and social behaviors at home. *Journal of Applied Psychology, 92*(5), 1368–1379. https://doi.org/10.1037/0021-9010.92.5.1368

Isaacs, E., A. Konrad, A. Walendowski, T. Lennig, V. Hollis, and S. Whittaker (2013). Echoes from the past: How technology mediated reflection improves well-being. In W. E. Mackay, S. Brewster, & S. Bødker (Eds.), *Proceedings of the SIGCHI conference on human factors in computing systems* (pp. 1071–1080). https://doi.org/10.1145/2470654.2466137

Ivonin, L., Chang, H.-M., Chen, W., & Rauterberg, M. (2013). Unconscious emotions: Quantifying and logging something we are not aware of. *Personal and Ubiquitous Computing, 17*(4), 663–673. https://doi.org/10.1007/s00779-012-0514-5

Jacquemard, T., Novitzky, P., O'Brolcháin, F., Smeaton, A. F., & Gordijn, B. (2014). Challenges and opportunities of lifelog technologies: A literature review and critical analysis. *Science and Engineering Ethics, 20*(2), 379–409. https://doi.org/10.1007/s11948-013-9456-1

Jalali, L., & Jain, R. (2013). Building health persona from personal data streams. In V. K. Singh, T. -S. Chua, R. Jain, & A. S. Pentland (Eds.), *Proceedings of the 1st ACM international workshop on Personal data meets distributed multimedia* (pp. 19–26). https://doi.org/10.1145/2509352.2509400

Johns, G. (2006). The essential impact of context on organizational behavior. *Academy of Management Review, 31*(2), 386–408. https://doi.org/10.5465/AMR.2006.20208687

Juslin, P. N., & Scherer, K. R. (2005). Vocal expression of affect. In J. A. Harrigan, R. Rosenthal, & K. R. Scherer (Eds.), *Series in affective science. The new handbook of methods in nonverbal behavior research* (pp. 65–135). New York: Oxford University Press.

Kahn, R. L., & Byosiere, P. (1992). Stress in organizations. In M. D. Dunnette & L. M. Hough (Eds.), *Handbook of industrial and organizational psychology* (Vol. 3, 2nd ed., pp. 571–650). Palo Alto, CA: Consulting Psychologists Press.

Kasl, S. V. (1978). Epidemiological contributions to the study of work stress. In C. L. Cooper & R. Payne (Eds.), *Wiley series on studies in occupational stress. Stress at work* (pp. 3–48). Chichester: Wiley.

Kelly, L., & Jones, G. J. F. (2009). Examining the utility of affective response in search of personal lifelogs. In *Proceedings of the 5th workshop on emotion in human-computer interaction.*

Kelly, P., Doherty, A. R., Berry, E., Hodges, S. E., Batterham, A. M., & Foster, C. (2011). Can we use digital life-log images to investigate active and sedentary travel behaviour? Results from a pilot study. *The International Journal of Behavioral Nutrition and Physical Activity 8*(44). https://doi.org/10.1186/1479-5868-8-44.

Kelly, P., Thomas, E., Doherty, A., Harms, T., Burke, O., Gershuny, J., & Foster, C. (2015). Developing a method to test the validity of 24 hour time use diaries using wearable cameras: A feasibility pilot. *PLoS One, 10*(12), e0142198. https://doi.org/10.1371/journal.pone.0142198

Kerr, J., Marshall, S. J., Godbole, S., Chen, J., Legge, A., Doherty, A. R., ... Foster, C. (2013). Using the SenseCam to improve classifications of sedentary behavior in free-living settings. *American Journal of Preventive Medicine, 44*(3), 290–296. https://doi.org/10.1016/j.amepre.2012.11.004

Khan, A. M., Siddiqi, M. H., & Lee, S.-W. (2013). Exploratory data analysis of acceleration signals to select light-weight and accurate features for real-time activity recognition on smartphones. *Sensors, 13*(10), 13099–13122. https://doi.org/10.3390/s131013099

Küller, R., Mikellides, B., & Janssens, J. (2009). Color, arousal, and performance—A comparison of three experiments. *Color Research & Application, 34*(2), 141–152. https://doi.org/10.1002/col.20476

Kumar, G., Jerbi, H., Gurrin, C., & O'Mahony, M. P. (2014). Towards activity recommendation from lifelogs. In M. Indrawan-Santiago, M. Steinbauer, H. -Q. Nguyen, A. M. Tjoa, I. Khalil, & G. Anderst-Kotsis (Eds.), *Proceedings of the 16th international conference on information integration and web-based applications & services* (pp. 87–96). https://doi.org/10.1145/2684200.2684298

Lazarus, R. S. (1966). *Psychological stress and the coping process*. New York: McGraw Hill.

Lazarus, R. S. (1990). Theory-based stress measurement. *Psychological Inquiry, 1*(1), 3–13.

Lazarus, R. S., & Folkman, S. (1984). *Stress, appraisal, and coping*. New York: Springer.

Lee, J.-M., Kim, Y., & Welk, G. J. (2014). Validity of consumer-based physical activity monitors. *Medicine and Science in Sports and Exercise, 46*(9), 1840–1848.

Lee, Y. -S., & Cho, S. -B. (2011). Activity recognition using hierarchical hidden Markov models on a smartphone with 3D accelerometer. In D. Hutchison, T. Kanade, J. Kittler, J. M. Kleinberg, F. Mattern, J. C. Mitchell, ... M. Woźniak (Eds.), *Lecture notes in computer science. Proceedings of the 6th international conference on hybrid artificial intelligent systems* (Vol. 6678, pp. 460–467). Berlin: Springer. https://doi.org/10.1007/978-3-642-21219-2_58

Lee, Y.-S., & Cho, S.-B. (2013). Mobile context inference using two-layered Bayesian networks for smartphones. *Expert Systems with Applications, 40*(11), 4333–4345. https://doi.org/10.1016/j.eswa.2013.01.018

Lee, Y.-S., & Cho, S.-B. (2014). Activity recognition with android phone using mixture-of-experts co-trained with labeled and unlabeled data. *Neurocomputing, 126*, 106–115. https://doi.org/10.1016/j.neucom.2013.05.044

Li, I., Dey, A. K., & Forlizzi, J. (2012). Using context to reveal factors that affect physical activity. *ACM Transactions on Computer-Human Interaction, 19*(1), 1–21. https://doi.org/10.1145/2147783.2147790

Li, N., Crane, M., Gurrin, C., & Ruskin, H. J. (2016). Finding motifs in large personal lifelogs. In A. Schmidt, T. Terada, W. Woo, P. Mistry, J. -M. Seigneur, J. M. Hernandez-Munoz, & P. McCullagh (Eds.), *Proceedings of the 7th augmented human international conference* (pp. 1–8). https://doi.org/10.1145/2875194.2875214

Lim, S., Lee, S.-H., & Cho, S.-B. (2016). A modular approach to landmark detection based on a Bayesian network and categorized context logs. *Information Sciences, 330*, 145–156. https://doi.org/10.1016/j.ins.2015.10.017

McDuff, D., Karlson, A., Kapoor, A., Roseway, A., & Czerwinski, M. (2012). AffectAura: An intelligent system for emotional memory. In: J. A. Konstan, E. H. Chi, & K. Höök (Eds.), *Proceedings of the ACM SIGCHI conference on human factors in computing systems* (pp. 849–858). https://doi.org/10.1145/2207676.2208525

McGrath, J. E. (1976). Stress and behavior in organizations. In M. D. Dunnette (Ed.), *Handbook of industrial and organizational psychology* (pp. 1351–1395). Chicago: Rand McNally College.

Miluzzo, E., Lane, N. D., Fodor, K., Peterson, R., Lu, H., Musolesi, M., ... Campbell, A. T. (2008). Sensing meets mobile social networks. In T. Abdelzaher, M. Martonosi, & A. Wolisz (Eds.), *Proceedings of the 6th ACM conference on embedded network sensor systems* (pp. 337–350). https://doi.org/10.1145/1460412.1460445

Mitchell, T. R., & James, L. R. (2001). Building better theory: Time and the specification of when things happen. *Academy of Management Review, 26*(4), 530–547. https://doi.org/10.5465/AMR.2001.5393889

Moen, P., Kelly, E. L., & Lam, J. (2013). Healthy work revisited: Do changes in time strain predict well-being? *Journal of Occupational Health Psychology, 18*(2), 157–172. https://doi.org/10.1037/a0031804

Monroe, S. M. (2008). Modern approaches to conceptualizing and measuring human life stress. *Annual Review of Clinical Psychology, 4*, 33–52. https://doi.org/10.1146/annurev.clinpsy.4.022007.141207

Mortazavi, B., Nemati, E., VanderWall, K., Flores-Rodriguez, H. G., Cai, J. Y. J., Lucier, J., ... Sarrafzadeh, M. (2015). Can smartwatches replace smartphones for posture tracking? *Sensors, 15*(10), 26783–26800. https://doi.org/10.3390/s151026783

Nielsen, K., & Randall, R. (2012). The importance of employee participation and perceptions of changes in procedures in a teamworking intervention. *Work and Stress, 26*(2), 91–111. https://doi.org/10.1080/02678373.2012.682721

Nielsen, K., Randall, R., & Albertsen, K. (2007). Participants' appraisals of process issues and the effects of stress management interventions. *Journal of Organizational Behavior, 28*(6), 793–810. https://doi.org/10.1002/job.450

Nunamaker, J. F., Derrick, D. C., Elkins, A. C., Burgoon, J. K., & Patton, M. W. (2011). Embodied conversational agent-based kiosk for automated interviewing. *Journal of Management Information Systems, 28*(1), 17–48. https://doi.org/10.2753/MIS0742-1222280102

Ohsawa, R., Takashio, K., & Tokuda, H. (2006). OreDesk: A tool for retrieving data history based on user operations. In IEEE (Ed.), *Proceedings of the 8th international symposium on multimedia (ISM 2006)* (pp. 762–765). https://doi.org/10.1109/ISM.2006.121

Oliver, M., Doherty, A. R., Kelly, P., Badland, H. M., Mavoa, S., Shepherd, J., ... Foster, C. (2013). Utility of passive photography to objectively audit built environment features of active transport journeys: An observational study. *International Journal of Health Geographics, 12*, 20. https://doi.org/10.1186/1476-072X-12-20

Paré, G., Trudel, M.-C., Jaana, M., & Kitsiou, S. (2015). Synthesizing information systems knowledge: A typology of literature reviews. *Information & Management, 52*(2), 183–199. https://doi.org/10.1016/j.im.2014.08.008

Parker, D. F., & DeCotiis, T. A. (1983). Organizational determinants of job stress. *Organizational Behavior and Human Performance, 32*, 160–177. https://doi.org/10.1016/0030-5073(83)90145-9

Pas, E. T., Bradshaw, C. P., & Hershfeldt, P. A. (2012). Teacher- and school-level predictors of teacher efficacy and burnout: Identifying potential areas for support. *Journal of School Psychology, 50*(1), 129–145. https://doi.org/10.1016/j.jsp.2011.07.003

Pearlin, L. I. (1989). The sociological study of stress. *Journal of Health and Social Behavior, 30*(3), 241–256. https://doi.org/10.2307/2136956

Perrewé, P. L., & Zellars, K. L. (1999). An examination of attributions and emotions in the transactional approach to the organizational stress process. *Journal of Organizational Behavior, 20*, 739–752. https://doi.org/10.1002/(SICI)1099-1379(199909)20:5<739::AID-JOB1949>3.0.CO;2-C

Petrou, P., Demerouti, E., & Schaufeli, W. B. (2015). Job crafting in changing organizations: Antecedents and implications for exhaustion and performance. *Journal of Occupational Health Psychology, 20*(4), 470–480. https://doi.org/10.1037/a0039003

Preece, S. J., Goulermas, J. Y., Kenney, L. P. J., Howard, D., Meijer, K., & Crompton, R. (2009). Activity identification using body-mounted sensors—A review of classification techniques. *Physiological Measurement, 30*(4), R1–R33. https://doi.org/10.1088/0967-3334/30/4/R01

Rai, A., Yan, Z., Chakraborty, D., Wijaya, T. K., & Aberer, K. (2012). Mining complex activities in the wild via a single smartphone accelerometer. In D. Das, A. R. Ganguly, V. Chandola, O. A. Omitaomu, K. Steinhaeuser, J. Gama, ... N. V. Chawla (Eds.), *Proceedings of the sixth international workshop on knowledge discovery from sensor data* (pp. 43–51). https://doi.org/10.1145/2350182.2350187

Reknes, I., Pallesen, S., Mageroy, N., Moen, B. E., Bjorvatn, B., & Einarsen, S. (2014). Exposure to bullying behaviors as a predictor of mental health problems among Norwegian nurses: Results from the prospective SUSSH-survey. *International Journal of Nursing Studies, 51*(3), 479–487. https://doi.org/10.1016/j.ijnurstu.2013.06.017

Riedl, R. (2013). On the biology of technostress: Literature review and research agenda. *DATA BASE for Advances in Information Systems, 44*(1), 18–55. https://doi.org/10.1145/2436239.2436242

Riedl, R., Davis, F. D., & Hevner, A. R. (2014). Towards a NeuroIS research methodology: Intensifying the discussion on methods, tools, and measurement. *Journal of the Association for Information Systems, 15*(10), i–xxxv.

Riedl, R., Kindermann, H., Auinger, A., & Javor, A. (2013). Computer breakdown as a stress factor during task completion under time pressure: Identifying gender differences based on skin conductance. *Advances in Human-Computer Interaction, 1*, 1–8.

Rizzuto, T. E., Mohammed, S., & Vance, R. J. (2011). Marching in-step: Facilitating technological transitions through climate consensus. *Computers in Human Behavior, 27*(1), 185–194. https://doi.org/10.1016/j.chb.2010.07.035

Ryoo, D.-W., & Bae, C. (2007). Design of the wearable gadgets for life-log services based on UTC. *IEEE Transactions on Consumer Electronics, 53*(4), 1477–1482. https://doi.org/10.1109/TCE.2007.4429240

Sanchez, J. I., & Viswesvaran, C. (2002). The effects of temporal separation on the relations between self-reported work stressors and strains. *Organizational Research Methods, 5*(2), 173–183. https://doi.org/10.1177/1094428102005002003

Sas, C., Fratczak, T., Rees, M., Gellersen, H., Kalnikaite, V., Coman, A., & Höök, K. (2013). AffectCam: Arousal-augmented SenseCam for richer recall of episodic memories. In: W. E. Mackay, S. Brewster, & S. Bødker (Eds.), *CHI '13 extended abstracts on human factors in computing systems* (pp. 1041–1046). https://doi.org/10.1145/2468356.2468542

Sellen, A. J., & Whittaker, S. (2010). Beyond total capture: A constructive critique of lifelogging. *Communications of the ACM, 53*(5), 70. https://doi.org/10.1145/1735223.1735243

Selye, H. (1936). A syndrome produced by diverse nocuous agents. *Nature, 138*(3479), 32. https://doi.org/10.1038/138032a0

Smith, A., O'Hara, K., & Lewis, P. (2011). Visualising the past: Annotating a life with linked open data. In: D. de Roure & S. Poole (Eds.), *Proceedings of the 3rd international web science conference* (pp. 1–8). https://doi.org/10.1145/2527031.2527038

Smith, B. K., Frost, J., Albayrak, M., & Sudhakar, R. (2007). Integrating glucometers and digital photography as experience capture tools to enhance patient understanding and communication of diabetes self-management practices. *Personal and Ubiquitous Computing, 11*(4), 273–286. https://doi.org/10.1007/s00779-006-0087-2

Sonnentag, S., & Frese, M. (2013). Stress in organizations. In I. B. Weiner & N. W. Schmitt (Eds.), *Handbook of psychology: Vol. 12. Handbook of psychology. Industrial and organizational psychology* (2nd ed., pp. 560–592). Hoboken, NJ: Wiley. https://doi.org/10.1002/0471264385.wei1218

Steptoe, A., Wardle, J., Lipsey, Z., Mills, R., Oliver, G., Jarvis, M., & Kirschbaum, C. (1998). A longitudinal study of work load and variations in psychological well-being, cortisol, smoking, and alcohol consumption. *Annals of Behavioral Medicine, 20*(2), 84–91. https://doi.org/10.1007/BF02884453

Stiglbauer, B., Selenko, E., Batinic, B., & Jodlbauer, S. (2012). On the link between job insecurity and turnover intentions: Moderated mediation by work involvement and well-being. *Journal of Occupational Health Psychology, 17*(3), 354–364. https://doi.org/10.1037/a0028565

Sun, L., Zhang, D., Li, B., Guo, B., & Li, S. (2010). Activity recognition on an accelerometer embedded mobile phone with varying positions and orientations. In: D. Hutchison, T. Kanade, J. Kittler, J. M. Kleinberg, F. Mattern, J. C. Mitchell, … X. Zhou (Eds.), *Lecture notes in computer science: Vol. 6406. Ubiquitous intelligence and computing* (Vol. 6406, pp. 548–562). Berlin: Springer. https://doi.org/10.1007/978-3-642-16355-5_42

Sun, L., Zhang, D., & Li, N. (2011). Physical activity monitoring with mobile phones. In D. Hutchison, T. Kanade, J. Kittler, J. M. Kleinberg, F. Mattern, J. C. Mitchell, et al. (Eds.), *Lecture notes in computer science: Vol. 6719. Toward useful services for elderly and people with disabilities* (Vol. 6719, pp. 104–111). Berlin: Springer. https://doi.org/10.1007/978-3-642-21535-3_14

Tams, S., Hill, K., de Guinea, A. O., Thatcher, J., & Grover, V. (2014). NeuroIS – Alternative or complement to existing methods? Illustrating the holistic effects of neuroscience and self-reported data in the context of technostress research. *Journal of the Association for Information Systems, 15*(Special Issue), 723–753.

Taraldsen, K., Askim, T., Sletvold, O., Einarsen, E. K., Bjåstad, K. G., Indredavik, B., & Helbostad, J. L. (2011). Evaluation of a body-worn sensor system to measure physical activity in older people with impaired function. *Physical Therapy, 91*(2), 277–285.

Terziyski, S., Albatal, R., & Gurrin, C. (2015). Fast human activity recognition in lifelogging. In X. He, S. Luo, D. Tao, C. Xu, J. Yang, & M. A. Hasan (Eds.), *Lecture notes in computer science: Vol. 8936. MultiMedia modeling* (Vol. 8936, pp. 369–379). Cham: Springer. https://doi.org/10.1016/j.patrec.2011.07.013

Torres-Huitzil, C., & Nuno-Maganda, M. (2015). Robust smartphone-based human activity recognition using a tri-axial accelerometer. In IEEE (Ed.), *Proceedings of the 6th Latin American symposium on circuits & systems (LASCAS 2015)* (pp. 1–4). https://doi.org/10.1109/LASCAS.2015.7250435

Tucker, W. J., Bhammar, D. M., Sawyer, B. J., Buman, M. P., & Gaesser, G. A. (2015). Validity and reliability of Nike + Fuelband for estimating physical activity energy expenditure. *BMC Sports Science, Medicine and Rehabilitation* *7*(14). https://doi.org/10.1186/s13102-015-0008-7

Tyson, P. D., & Pongruengphant, R. (2004). Five-year follow-up study of stress among nurses in public and private hospitals in Thailand. *International Journal of Nursing Studies, 41*(3), 247–254. https://doi.org/10.1016/S0020-7489(03)00134-2

Van der Elst, T., Richter, A., Sverke, M., Naeswall, K., Cuyper, N. de, & Witte, H. de (2014). Threat of losing valued job features: The role of perceived control in mediating the effect of qualitative job insecurity on job strain and psychological withdrawal. *Work and Stress 28*(2), 143–164. https://doi.org/10.1080/02678373.2014.899651

Vemuri, S., & Bender, W. (2004). Next-generation personal memory aids. *BT Technology Journal, 22*(4), 125–138. https://doi.org/10.1023/B:BTTJ.0000047591.29175.89

Vemuri, S., Schmandt, C., & Bender, W. (2006). iRemember: A personal, long-term memory prosthesis. In K. Mase (Ed.), *Proceedings of the 3rd ACM workshop on continuous archival and retrieval of personal experiences* (pp. 65–74). https://doi.org/10.1145/1178657.1178670

Venkatesh, V., Brown, S. A., & Bala, H. (2013). Bridging the qualitative-quantitative divide: Guidelines for conducting mixed methods research in information systems. *MIS Quarterly, 37* (1), 21–54.

Venkatesh, V., Brown, S. A., & Sullivan, Y. W. (2016). Guidelines for conducting mixed-methods research: An extension and illustration. *Journal of the Association for Information Systems, 7* (17), 435–494.

Vischer, J. C. (2007). The effects of the physical environment on job performance: Towards a theoretical model of workspace stress. *Stress and Health, 23*, 175–184.

Vrijkotte, T. G. M., van Doornen, L. J. P., & de Geus, E. J. C. (2000). Effects of work stress on ambulatory blood pressure, heart rate, and heart rate variability. *Hypertension, 35*(4), 880–886. https://doi.org/10.1161/01.HYP.35.4.880

Wang, P., & Smeaton, A. F. (2013). Using visual lifelogs to automatically characterize everyday activities. *Information Sciences, 230*, 147–161. https://doi.org/10.1016/j.ins.2012.12.028

Wang, P., Sun, L., Yang, S., Smeaton, A., & Gurrin, C. (2016). Characterizing everyday activities from visual lifelogs based on enhancing concept representation. *Computer Vision and Image Understanding, 148*, 181–192. https://doi.org/10.1016/j.cviu.2015.09.014

Weiss, G. M., Timko, J. L., Gallagher, C. M., Yoneda, K., & Schreiber, A. J. (2016). Smartwatch-based activity recognition: A machine learning approach. In *Proceedings of the IEEE-EMBS international conference on biomedical and health informatics (BHI)* (pp. 426–429). https://doi.org/10.1109/BHI.2016.7455925

Weiss, M. (1983). Effects of work stress and social support on information systems managers. *MIS Quarterly, 7*(1), 29. https://doi.org/10.2307/249075

Whittaker, S., Tucker, S., Swampillai, K., & Laban, R. (2008). Design and evaluation of systems to support interaction capture and retrieval. *Personal and Ubiquitous Computing, 12*(3), 197–221. https://doi.org/10.1007/s00779-007-0146-3

Wolf, K., Schmidt, A., Bexheti, A., & Langheinrich, M. (2014). Lifelogging: You're wearing a camera? *IEEE Pervasive Computing, 13*(3), 8–12.

Wu, H., Lemaire, E. D., & Baddour, N. (2012). Activity change-of-state identification using a Blackberry smartphone. *Journal of Medical and Biological Engineering, 32*(4), 265. https://doi.org/10.5405/jmbe.967

Zapf, D., Dormann, C., & Frese, M. (1996). Longitudinal studies in organizational stress research: A review of the literature with reference to methodological issues. *Journal of Occupational Health Psychology, 1*(2), 145–169. https://doi.org/10.1037/1076-8998.1.2.145

Zhang, S., McCullagh, P., Zhang, J., & Yu, T. (2014). A smartphone based real-time daily activity monitoring system. *Cluster Computing, 17*(3), 711–721. https://doi.org/10.1007/s10586-013-0335-y

Appendix

1 Review of Limitations in Longitudinal OS Research

We conducted a literature review to identify the main limitations related to capture, retrieval, and the dynamic aspects of stress featured in longitudinal OS publications conducted since the publication of a methodological paper by Zapf, Dormann, and Frese (1996). For this purpose, we adhered to the following procedure. We used the combination "Stress" (Topic) AND "Organization*" (Topic) AND "Longitudinal" (Topic) to search for relevant journal publications in the Web of Science (last search on 08/25/2016). This initial research led to 548 results, which we then refined by only including publications from 1997 to 2016 and the document types "Article" and "Review". This refinement resulted in 463 journal publications eligible for an initial selection, based on the publication title. Reviewing the retrieved publications based on title led to another 188 entries being excluded from further review.

We then screened the abstracts of the 275 remaining publications based on three main criteria. First, we checked whether these publications were related to OS, though in a wider sense (i.e., research conducted with individuals in their roles as organizational members, focusing on at least one stressor and individual strain, such as workload as potential stressor and absenteeism as potential strain). Here, we also reviewed the used samples and decided to exclude studies which used student samples (3 studies) in addition to those studies which were not related to OS (89 studies). In a second step, we reviewed whether the remaining studies were empirical studies. Here, we excluded studies which did not collect any data (14 studies), but also studies which only analyzed previously collected data (8 studies) or only collected data to test a newly developed measurement instrument (3 studies). Finally, we checked whether the remaining studies had actually adopted a longitudinal study design, based on their abstracts, but also their full text later on, which led to an additional 27 studies being excluded from our review.

T. Fischer, R. Riedl, *Lifelogging for Organizational Stress Measurement*,
SpringerBriefs in Information Systems,
https://doi.org/10.1007/978-3-319-98711-8_2

As we were still left with 130 generally relevant publications at this point, we decided to implement a quality criterion to leave us with only the most rigorous studies in order to identify only the most pressing methodological limitations during our review. Thus, we aimed for a convenience sample of around 50 studies published in the highest impact journals. For this selection, we reviewed the impact of journals these 130 studies had been published in (http://www.scimagojr.com/—08/27/2016; see Table 1) and decided to focus on journals with a 2-year impact factor of at least 3.00. For our review we therefore ended up with 50 publications, as listed in Table 2 (chronological order).

2 Review of Lifelogging Publications

In order to identify publications suitable for our review of lifelogging research, we first used the term "lifelog*" in Google Scholar (06/01/2017: 5750 hits) and selected journal publications as well as publications in scientific periodicals which had accumulated more than five citations thus far.[1] We chose to search for articles in Google Scholar, due to the Web of Science only offering a very limited selection of lifelogging publications at this point (i.e., searching for "lifelog*" as a topic resulted in only 66 journal publications). We reviewed all publications among these 5750 hits and selected suitable publications based on their publishing outlet, number of citations, as well as a review of their title and abstract. These criteria led to a set of 98 publications which we then skimmed through, and excluded another 29 publications as they did not offer sufficient information on the types of data involved (e.g., in the case of empirical studies or tool concepts). Two additional articles were excluded as one only involved paper-based logging of information and the other one involved the collection of personal health information, though only for the use of medical personnel (i.e., a form of monitoring, hence not an application of individual lifelogging).[2] To further check for important publications we searched in the repositories of the journals that these papers had been published in,[3] but identified no additional publications.

[1]A similar criterion has previously been applied in a literature review by Riedl (2013).

[2]It has to be noted that we do not claim that the 69 publications which we identified constitute an exhaustive list of available publications.

[3]ACM T Embed Comput S; Am J Prev Med; Appl Intell; Biomed Eng Online; BT Technol J; Commun ACM; Comput Hum Behav; Educ Technol Soc; Euro J Clin Nutr; Expert Syst Appl; Hum-Centr Com Inf Sc; Hum-Comput Interact; IEEE Multimedia; IEEE Pervasive Comput; IEEE T Consum Electr; IEEE T Multimedia; Inform Sciences; Inform Syst; Int J Behav Nutr Phys Act; Int J Computer Healthc; Int J Distrib Sens N; Int J Hum-Comput St; Int J Multimed Inf Retr; ITE T Media Tech Appl; J Amb Intel Smart En; J Cognitive Neurosci; J Electr Eng Comput Eng; J Med Biol Eng; J Neurol Neurosurg Ps; J Sensor Actuator Netw; Med Eng Phys; Memory; Mobile Netw Appl; Multimedia Syst; Multimed Tools Appl; Neuropsychol Rehabil; Pers Ubiquit Comput; Res Prac Technol Enhanc Learn; Sensors.

Table 1 Overview of journals and impact for our preliminary sample of 130 studies

Journal name	No. of studies	Impact 08/27/2016
Journals/Studies included in review		
Academy of Management Journal	1	6.4
Journal of Management	1	6.07
Organizational Research Methods	1	5.75
Annals of Family Medicine	1	5.06
Sleep	1	4.89
American Journal of Epidemiology	1	4.52
Personnel Psychology	3	4.41
American Sociological Review	1	4.38
Journal of Applied Psychology	5	3.95
Annals of Behavioral Medicine	1	3.87
International Journal of Nursing Studies	4	3.79
Computers in Human Behavior	1	3.61
Scandinavian Journal of Work Environment and Health	2	3.57
Journal of Organizational Behavior	1	3.27
Work and Stress	11	3.26
Journal of School Psychology	1	3.18
Journal of Health Psychology	1	3.11
Journal of Occupational Health Psychology	10	3.11
Human Relations	2	3.06
Environment and Behavior	1	3.02
Journals/Studies excluded from review		
Social Science and Medicine	1	2.99
Journal of Vocational Behavior	3	2.89
British Journal of Management	1	2.78
Journal of Service Research	1	2.78
European Journal of Public Health	1	2.64
International Journal of Hospitality Management	2	2.62
European Journal of Work and Organizational Psychology	2	2.41
Journal of Occupational and Organizational Psychology	4	2.39
BMC Public Health	1	2.38
Asia Pacific Journal of Management	1	2.35
Journal of Health and Social Behavior	1	2.26
Journal of Research in Personality	1	2.26
Accident Analysis and Prevention	1	2.25
International Journal of Environmental Research and Public Health	1	2.21
Frontiers in Psychology	2	2.2
Group and Organization Management	1	2.02
International Journal of Human Computer Interaction	2	1.93
BMC Health Services Research	1	1.92
International Journal of Stress Management	1	1.81

(continued)

Table 1 (continued)

Journal name	No. of studies	Impact 08/27/ 2016
American Journal of Industrial Medicine	1	1.79
Psychological Trauma—Theory, Research and Practice	1	1.79
International Archives of Occupational and Environmental Health	2	1.77
Journal of Nursing Management	2	1.77
Disability and Rehabilitation	1	1.71
Maternal and Child Health Journal	1	1.71
Human Factors	1	1.71
International Journal of Behavioral Medicine	1	1.64
Psychological Services	1	1.64
Anxiety, Stress and Coping	1	1.61
Stress and Health	7	1.57
Journal of Occupational and Environmental Medicine	2	1.54
Nursing Ethics	1	1.5
Career Development International	1	1.44
British Journal of General Practice	1	1.43
Scandinavian Journal of Psychology	1	1.43
Journal of Managerial Psychology	1	1.42
Qualitative Health Research	1	1.37
Health Promotion International	1	1.36
Disability and Health Journal	1	1.35
Journal of Social and Clinical Psychology	1	1.33
Industrial Health	3	1.26
Asian Journal of Social Psychology	1	1.24
International Journal of Industrial Ergonomics	1	1.24
Scandinavian Journal of Public Health	2	1.2
Journal of Occupational Health	2	1.17
Children and Youth Services Review	2	1.13
Journal of Applied Social Psychology	4	1.08
Occupational Medicine Oxford	1	1.05
Journal of Personnel Psychology	1	1.03
Economic and Industrial Democracy	1	0.88
Journal of Healthcare Management	1	0.8
Work	1	0.7
Canadian Journal of Administrative Sciences	1	0.68
Military Psychology	1	0.67

These "landmark publications" (i.e., publications which have significantly influenced the research domain, as indicated by their number of citations, see Table 3) were then used as input for the next stage of our review. We again used Google Scholar for a forward search, using the combined citations of the previously selected publications as input (Google Scholar: 07/05/2017; forward search based on

Table 2 Overview of selected publications and their main attributes (N = 50)

Study	Main methods of data capture	Measurement points	Lag(s)
Moyle (1998)	Surveys	Three	6 months & 6 months
Steptoe et al. (1998)	Surveys Saliva samples	Four	1–2 months
Brennan, Chugh, and Kline (2002)	Surveys Interviews Focus Groups	Three	1 month & 5 months
Fugate, Kinicki, and Scheck (2002)	Surveys	Four	3 months (between each wave)
Sanchez and Viswesvaran (2002)	Surveys	Two	60 days
Bravo, Peiro, Rodriguez, and Whitely (2003)	Surveys Interviews	Two	2 years
Korunka, Scharitzer, Carayon, and Sainfort (2003)	Surveys	Two	Several months
Croon, Sluiter, Blonk, Broersen, and Frings-Dresen (2004)	Surveys	Two	2 years
Jimmieson, Terry, and Callan (2004)	Surveys	Two	2 years
Tyson and Pongruengphant (2004)	Surveys	Two	5 years
Amiot, Terry, Jimmieson, and Callan (2006)	Surveys	Two	2 years
Edwards, Guppy, and Cockerton (2007)	Surveys	Two	3 months
Ilies, Schwind, Wagner, and Johnson (2007)	Surveys Interviews	Duration: Two weeks	Three times daily
Nielsen, Randall, and Albertsen (2007)	Surveys	Two	20 months
Elo and Ervasti (2008)	Surveys	Two	2 years
Fugate, Kinicki, and Prussia (2008)	Surveys Secondary data	Two	12 months
Hansson, Vingard, Arnetz, and Anderzen (2008)	Surveys Blood samples Secondary data	Two	12 months
Maslach and Leiter (2008)	Surveys	Two	12 months
Xie, Schaubroeck, and Lam (2008)	Surveys Blood samples Blood pressure	Two	2 years
Galais and Moser (2009)	Surveys	Three	5 months & 14 months
Bragard, Etienne, Merckaert, Libert, and Razavi (2010)	Surveys	Two	2 months
Grau-Alberola, Gil-Monte, Garcia-Juesas, and Figueiredo-Ferraz (2010)	Surveys	Two	12 months
Hoobler, Rospenda, Lemmon, and Rosa (2010)	Surveys	Two	12 months

(continued)

Table 2 (continued)

Study	Main methods of data capture	Measurement points	Lag(s)
Diestel and Schmidt (2011)	Survey (Study 2) Secondary data	Two	24 months
Finne, Knardahl, and Lau (2011)	Surveys	Two	2 years
Hyvonen, Feldt, Kinnunen, and Tolvanen (2011)	Surveys	Two	2 years
Lang, Bliese, Lang, and Adler (2011)	Surveys	Sample 1:	
		Two	7 months
		Sample 2:	
		Two	3 months
Rizzuto, Mohammed, and Vance (2011)	Surveys Interviews Secondary data	Six	12 months (between each point)
Wang, Zhan, McCune, and Truxillo (2011)	Surveys	Two	3 months
Childs and Stoeber (2012)	Surveys	Sample 1:	
		Two	6 months
		Sample 2:	
		Two	3 months
Nielsen and Randall (2012)	Surveys	Two	18 months
Nielsen, Hetland, Matthiesen, and Einarsen (2012)	Surveys	Two	2 years
Pas, Bradshaw, and Hershfeldt (2012)	Surveys	Three	6 months & 12 months
Stiglbauer, Selenko, Batinic, and Jodlbauer (2012)	Surveys	Two	6 months
Wang, Patten, Currie, Sareen, and Schmitz (2012)	Surveys	Two	12 months
Yang, Spector, Chang, Gallant-Roman, and Powell (2012)	Surveys	Two	6 months
Bono, Glomb, Shen, Kim, and Koch (2013)	Surveys Interviews Blood pressure	Duration: Three weeks	Daily: 4 surveys 1 interview
Brough et al. (2013)	Surveys	Two	12 months
Moen, Kelly, and Lam (2013)	Surveys	Two	6 months
Odle-Dusseau et al. (2013)	Surveys	Two	3 months
Alidina, Rosenthal, Schneider, Singer, and Friedberg (2014)	Surveys Interviews	Two Three	30 months 18 months & 12 months
Biggs, Brough, and Barbour (2014)	Surveys	Three	18 months & 12 months
Hanson, Chungkham, Akerstedt, and Westerlund (2014)	Surveys	Two	2 years

(continued)

Table 2 (continued)

Study	Main methods of data capture	Measurement points	Lag(s)
Idris, Dollard, and Yulita (2014)	Surveys	Two	3 months
Naeswall, Sverke, and Goeransson (2014)	Surveys	Three	12 months & 12 months
Reknes et al. (2014)	Surveys	Two	12 months
Vander Elst et al. (2014)	Surveys	Two	14 months
Elovainio et al. (2015)	Surveys	Two	4 years
Petrou, Demerouti, and Schaufeli (2015)	Surveys	Two	12 months
Moen et al. (2016)	Surveys	Three	6 months & 6 months

69 publications and 4299 combined citations). We selected studies that have been published in peer-reviewed journals as well as conference proceedings, but only focused on those that have applied off-the-shelf devices for collection (i.e., commercially available, consumer-grade devices, such as smartphones, smartwatches, wearable cameras, or fitness trackers). This selection led to 86 publications being included in the extension of our review.

In Table 3 we have listed the combined 155 lifelogging publications in our review as well as the combined classification of the data sources that have been involved and the inferences, relevant for OS research, that have been made. We indicated studies that only collected data, but made no inferences at all, or none that were relevant for OS, by entering “n/a” in the column “OS Research”.

3 Review of Lifelogging Tools

We used the “Quantified Self—Guide to Self-Tracking Tools” (http://quantifiedself.com/guide/tools/) to identify further tools which are potentially relevant for stress research. We used the keywords “stress”, “arousal” and “emotion” to lookup suitable tools based on their title or description on 07/16/2017. As seen in Table 4, this procedure led to the identification of ten tools for “stress”, as well as two additional tools for “arousal” and another six additional tools for “emotion”. This list of 505 tools arguably constitutes the largest database of devices and applications that can be used for lifelogging purposes. We checked for the current availability of each tool and, in addition to describing their purpose and classifying captured data and their potential for OS research, we highlighted those tools that are not available anymore at the end of Table 5.

Table 3 Overview of 155 lifelogging studies in our review and results of classification

Studies	Citations (07/02/2016)	OS Research						Lifelogging			
		Input			Output						
		Task	Social	Physical	Psychological	Physiological	Behavioral	Individual	Environment	Device-specific	Third Party
Landmark Publications (N = 69)—Retrieval Date: 06/01/2017											
Vemuri and Bender (2004)	46			X					X	X	X
Blum, Pentland, and Troster (2006)	101	X	X	X	X	X	X	X	X	X	
Gemmell, Bell, and Lueder (2006)	580	n/a						X	X	X	X
Anderson et al. (2007)	221					X	X			X	
Berry et al. (2007)	191	–							X		
Cho, Kim, Hwang, and Song (2007)	63	X	X	X		X	X		X	X	X
Silva, Yamasaki, and Aizawa (2007)	39		X	X			X		X		
Kawamura, Fukuhara, Takeda, Kono, and Kidode (2007)	46			X	X				X		
Kern, Schiele, and Schmidt (2007)	112		X	X	X		X	X	X		
Ryoo and Bae (2007)	29			X				X	X		
Smith, Frost, Albayrak, and Sudhakar (2007)	82					X	X	X	X		

Wu et al. (2007)	40			X				X	X	X	
Choudhury et al. (2008)	511		X	X		X	X	X	X		
Lee et al. (2008)	83	n/a							X		
Ogata, Misumi, Matsuka, El-Bishouty, and Yano (2008)	17	n/a							X		
Whittaker, Tucker, Swampillai, and Laban (2008)	56	n/a							X		
Abe, Morinishi, Maeda, Aoki, and Inagaki (2009)	36	X		X		X	X	X	X		
Berry et al. (2009)	55	n/a							X		
Gyorbiro, Fabian, and Hományi (2009)	205					X	X	X	X	X	
Hwang and Cho (2009)	44	X	X	X	X	X	X		X	X	X
Byrne, Doherty, Snoek, Jones, and Smeaton (2010)	45	X	X	X		X	X		X		
Doherty and Smeaton (2010)	36			X				X	X		X
Kikhia, Hallberg, Bengtsson, Savenstedt, and Synnes (2010)	32		X	X			X		X		

(continued)

Table 3 (continued)

Studies	Citations (07/02/ 2016)	OS Research						Lifelogging			
		Input			Output						
		Task	Social	Physical	Psychological	Physiological	Behavioral	Individual	Environment	Device-specific	Third Party
Whittaker, Bergman, and Clough (2010)	110	n/a							X		
Brindley, Bateman, and Gracey (2011)	33	n/a						X	X		
Browne et al. (2011)	49	n/a							X		
Choi et al. (2011)	25		X	X			X		X		
Doherty, Caprani, et al. (2011)	89	X	X	X		X	X		X		
Doherty, Moulin, and Smeaton (2011)	61		X		X				X		
Hodges, Berry, and Wood (2011)	115	n/a							X		
Jacques, Conway, Lowder, and Cabeza (2011)	60	n/a							X		
Kalnikaite and Whittaker (2011)	29	n/a						X	X		
Kelly et al. (2011)	87	n/a							X		
Lee and Cho (2011b)	12		X	X	X		X		X	X	X
Lee, Khan, and Kim (2011)	59					X	X	X			
Lindley, Glancy, Harper, Randall, and Smyth (2011)	20	n/a						X	X		

Ogata et al. (2011)	97			X	X			X	X		
Park and Cho (2011)	14	X	X	X	X		X		X		
Park, Oh, and Cho (2011)	21		X	X	X		X		X	X	X
Pauly-Takacs, Moulin, and Estlin (2011)	35	n/a							X		
Doherty et al. (2012)	63		X		X				X		
Teraoka (2012)	45	n/a						X	X	X	
Wang and Smeaton (2012)	19	n/a						X	X		
Whittaker et al. (2012)	46	n/a						X	X		
Wu, Lemaire, and Baddour (2012)	17					X	X	X	X		
Aizawa (2013)	13						X		X		
Aizawa et al. (2013)	34						X		X		
Gemming, Doherty, Kelly, Utter, and Ni Mhurchu (2013)	41	X	X	X		X	X	X	X		
Gurrin et al. (2013)	45	X	X	X		X	X		X	X	
Ivonin, Chang, Chen, and Rauterberg (2013)	35					X		X	X		
Kang, Moudon, Hurvitz, Reichley, and Saelens (2013)	49			X			X	X	X		

(continued)

Table 3 (continued)

Studies	Citations (07/02/2016)	OS Research						Lifelogging			
		Input			Output						
		Task	Social	Physical	Psychological	Physiological	Behavioral	Individual	Environment	Device-specific	Third Party
Nam, Rho, and Lee (2013)	17			X		X	X	X	X		
Rawassizadeh, Tomitsch, Wac, and Tjoa (2013)	53		X					X	X	X	
Wang and Smeaton (2013)	33	X	X	X		X	X	X	X		
Wu, Zhu, and Zhang (2013)	36	X	X	X			X	X	X	X	
Han, Bang, Nugent, McClean, and Lee (2014)	12			X			X	X	X		
Hussain et al. (2014)	12			X			X	X	X	X	
Ogata et al. (2014)	28				X			X	X		
Aizawa and Ogawa (2015)	11						X		X		
Fida et al. (2015)	14						X	X			
Mafrur, Nugraha, and Choi (2015)	10		X	X			X	X	X	X	
Mortazavi et al. (2015)	10					X	X	X			
Rawassizadeh, Momeni, Dobbins, Mirza-Babaei, and Rahnamoun (2015)	6	n/a						X	X	X	

Rawassizadeh, Tomitsch, et al. (2015)	17			X		X	X	X	X	X	
Zheng (2015)	10			X			X	X	X		
Amin et al. (2016)	8					X	X	X	X		
Banos, Bilal Amin, et al. (2016)	13					X	X	X	X		
Chahuara et al. (2016)	6		X	X			X	X	X		
Palumbo, Gallicchio, Pucci, and Micheli (2016)	10			X		X	X	X	X	X	
∑ (Citations): 4299	∑	11	22	33	11	22	39	34	65	19	7

Extension for State-of-the-Art Research (N = 86)—Retrieval Dates: 07/05/2017

	Task	Social	Physical	Psychological	Physiological	Behavioral	Individual	Environment	Device-specific	Third Party
Ohsawa, Takashio, and Tokuda (2006)				X		X				
Vemuri, Schmandt, and Bender (2006)		X						X		
Bicocchi, Castelli, Mamei, Rosi, and Zambonelli (2008)			X					X		
Byrne et al. (2008)	X					X		X		
Doherty, Ó Conaire, Blighe, Smeaton, and O'Connor (2008)	n/a							X		
Harper et al. (2008)	n/a							X		
Miluzzo et al. (2008)		X	X		X	X	X	X	X	
Puangpakisiri, Yamasaki, and Aizawa (2008)	X		X		X	X	X	X	X	
Kelly and Jones (2009)				X	X		X	X		

(continued)

Table 3 (continued)

Extension for State-of-the-Art Research (N = 86)—Retrieval Dates: 07/05/2017

	Task	Social	Physical	Psychological	Physiological	Behavioral	Individual	Environment	Device-specific	Third Party
Bao and Choudhury (2010)		X		X		X	X	X		
Berchtold, Budde, Gordon, Schmidtke, and Beigl (2010)					X	X	X			
Chen and Jones (2010)	n/a						X	X	X	X
Ganti, Srinivasan, and Gacic (2010)	X	X	X		X	X	X	X		
Kwapisz, Weiss, and Moore (2010)					X	X	X			
Sun, Zhang, Li, Guo, and Li (2010)					X	X	X			
Zhang, McCullagh, Nugent, and Zheng (2010)					X	X	X			
Chen, Jones, and Debasis (2011)	n/a							X	X	
Jacques, Conway, and Cabeza (2011)	n/a							X		
Lee and Cho (2011a)					X	X	X			
Loveday and Conway (2011)								X		
Murphy, Barnard, Terry, Carthery-Goulart, and Holmes (2011)	n/a							X		
Qiu, Doherty, Gurrin, and Smeaton (2011)					X	X	X			
Smith, O'Hara, and Lewis (2011)		X	X					X	X	
Sun, Zhang, and Li (2011)					X	X	X			
Wang and Smeaton (2011)				X				X		

Albert, Toledo, Shapiro, and Kording (2012)					X	X	X			
Anguita, Ghio, Oneto, Parra, and Reyes-Ortiz (2012)					X	X	X			
Dobbins, Merabti, Fergus, and Llewellyn-Jones (2012)							X	X		
Hou, Ogata, Li, and Uosaki (2012)	n/a							X		
Pernek, Stiglic, and Kokol (2012)					X	X	X			
Rai et al. (2012)	X	X	X		X	X	X			
Anjum and Ilyas (2013)					X	X	X			
Chen et al. (2013)	X	X	X		X	X		X		
Derawi and Bours (2013)					X	X	X			
Doherty et al. (2013)	X	X	X		X	X	X	X		
Gouveia and Karapanos (2013)	n/a						X	X	X	
Isaacs et al. (2013)	n/a						X	X		
Jalali and Jain (2013)	X	X	X		X	X	X	X	X	X
Kerr et al. (2013)					X	X	X			
Khan, Siddiqi, and Lee (2013)					X	X	X			
Lee and Cho (2013)	X	X	X		X	X		X	X	
Marinac et al. (2013)					X	X		X		
Martín, Bernardos, Iglesias, and Casar (2013)					X	X	X	X		
Oliver et al. (2013)			X		X	X		X		
Otebolaku and Andrade (2013)					X	X	X			
Sas et al. (2013)					X		X	X		
Dobbins, Merabti, Fergus, and Llewellyn-Jones (2014)			X		X	X	X	X		

(continued)

Table 3 (continued)

Extension for State-of-the-Art Research (N = 86)—Retrieval Dates: 07/05/2017

	Task	Social	Physical	Psychological	Physiological	Behavioral	Individual	Environment	Device-specific	Third Party
Hu, Smeaton, and Newman (2014)					X	X	X			
Jeon, Yeon, Lee, and Seo (2014)	n/a						X	X	X	
Kelly et al. (2014)					X	X		X		
Kikhia et al. (2014)			X			X		X		
Kumar, Jerbi, Gurrin, and O'Mahony (2014)						X		X		
Lee and Cho (2014)			X		X	X	X	X		
Lockhart and Weiss (2014)					X	X	X			
Moghimi et al. (2014)			X		X	X		X		
Okamoto and Yanai (2014)					X	X		X		
Wang, Smeaton, Zhang, and Deng (2014)	X		X		X	X		X		
Zhang, McCullagh, Zhang, and Yu (2014)					X	X	X			
Albayram and Khan (2015)		X	X			X		X	X	
Chowdhury, McParlane, Ferdous, and Jose (2015)	n/a							X		
Gemming, Doherty, Utter, Shields, and Ni Mhurchu (2015)		X	X		X	X		X		
Güldenpfennig and Fitzpatrick (2015)	n/a						X	X	X	
Huang et al. (2015)			X			X	X	X		X
Kelly et al. (2015)	X	X	X		X	X		X		
Kim, Lee, Kim, and Kim (2015)					X	X	X			

Saeedi and El-Sheimy (2015)			X		X	X	X	X		
Terziyski, Albatal, and Gurrin (2015)	X	X	X		X	X		X		
Torres-Huitzil and Nuno-Maganda (2015)					X	X	X			
Banos, Villalonga, et al. (2016)				X	X	X	X	X		
Cho (2016)			X			X		X	X	
Connor, McCaffrey, Whyte, and Moran (2016)	n/a						X	X		
Ellis, Kerr, Godbole, Staudenmayer, and Lanckriet (2016)					X	X	X			
Faye, Louveton, Gheorghe, and Engel (2016)			X		X	X	X	X	X	
Lee and Cho (2016)					X	X	X	X		
Li, Crane, Gurrin, and Ruskin (2016)	n/a							X		
Lim, Lee, and Cho (2016)	n/a						X	X	X	
Merler, Wu, Uceda-Sosa, Nguyen, and Smith (2016)					X	X		X		
Nishiyama et al. (2016)	n/a						X			
Otebolaku and Andrade (2016)			X		X	X	X	X		
Safadi, Mulhem, Quenot, and Chevallet (2016)	n/a							X		
San-Segundo, Lorenzo-Trueba, Martínez-González, and Pardo (2016)			X		X	X	X			
Shoaib, Bosch, Incel, Scholten, and Havinga (2016)	X	X	X		X	X	X			

(continued)

Table 3 (continued)

Extension for State-of-the-Art Research (N = 86)—Retrieval Dates: 07/05/2017

	Task	Social	Physical	Psychological	Physiological	Behavioral	Individual	Environment	Device-specific	Third Party
Wang, Sun, Yang, Smeaton, and Gurrin (2016)	X	X	X		X	X		X		
Weiss, Timko, Gallagher, Yoneda, and Schreiber (2016)			X		X	X	X			
Hur, Bang, Kim, Banos, and Lee (2017)			X		X	X	X	X		
Pendergast, Ridgers, Worsley, and McNaughton (2017)	n/a						X	X		
Σ	13	16	30	5	54	60	55	64	19	6

Table 4 Keywords used and results for lifelogging tools

1. "Stress" 10 tools	2. "Arousal" 2 new tools	3. "Emotion" 6 new tools
Azumio: Stress Check Stress Doctor Instant Heart Rate Basis HR Monitor Watch Cataphora's Digital Mirror HeartMath: emWave2 Heart Wizard Mequilibrium MyBreath StressEraser Stresswatch	MindMetrics Rationalizer	AffectCheck AnalyzeWords BodyMonitor GottaFeeling MyMoodMap Pepfly

Table 5 Additional lifelogging tools for OS-related capture

Tool overview	Description (http://quantifiedself.com/guide/)
AnalyzeWords[a] Tool Type: Online service Data Type: Device-specific (tweets) Potential Use: Psychological Outputs	"AnalyzeWords is a service that performs linguistic analysis on any Twitter account in order to reveal the user's personality. Personality is broken down into emotional style (upbeat to depressed), social style ("plugged in" to "spacy valley girl"), and thinking style ("analytic" to "in-the-moment".) The analysis is performed by analyzing the usually unnoticed text of "junk words", such as articles, pronouns, and prepositions."
Azumio: Stress Check[b]; Stress Doctor[c]; Instant Heart Rate[d] Tool Type: Software (mobile apps) Data Type: Individual (Physiological data: HRV via PPG through camera) Potential Use: Physiological Outputs	"Azumio is dedicated to improving people's health and wellness by influencing behavior through the use of innovative mobile applications. Their apps are Stress Check, Stress Doctor, and Instant Heart Rate, which use the iPhone 4 camera to measure heart rate."
BodyMonitor[e] Tool Type: Wearable device (armband) Data Type: Individual (skin conductance, skin temperature, motion, Environment (magnetic fields, ambient temperature) Potential Use: Psychological Output (emotion), Physiological Output	"BodyMonitor is a research tool used by the GESIS (http://www.gesis.org) Leibniz-Institut for Sozialwissenschaft (Institute for Social Intelligence). The monitor is a wearable armband, measuring heart rate and skin conductance, and is used also to assess emotional state. It uses AI and biometric data to assess the emotional state of the user. It is primarily a research platform and has been used for assessing emotional states of people in urban settings."

(continued)

Table 5 (continued)

Tool overview	Description (http://quantifiedself.com/guide/)
Cataphora[f] Tool Type: Software (PC, Laptop) Data Type: Device-specific (e-mail) Potential Use: Social Context	"Cataphora's Digital Mirror is a tool for analyzing your email to learn about your social habits. It is based on Elizabeth Charnrock's book, E-Habits. The key idea is using email context to infer information about social habits. It is intended for work relationships, and features analysis of who you spent the most time with in emails as well as in person (inferring meetings), what topics with whom have been stressful, and what social hierarchies exist (. . .)."
GottaFeeling[g] Tool Type: Software (mobile app) Data Type: Individual (diary with self-report) Potential Use: Psychological Outputs	"GottaFeeling is a free iPhone app that is designed to help you record your feelings. It offers a menu of feelings to help users identify their emotions, and allows them to be shared via email, twitter, or facebook, as well as logged along with location and time. The application will produce various reports of feelings, and advanced reporting is available for an upgrade."
HeartMath: emWave2[h] Tool Type: Hardware (Handheld device) Data Type: Individual (Physiological data: HRV via PPG through ear sensor) Potential Use: Physiological Outputs	"HeartMath provides tools for monitoring heart rate variability, along with software, books, and audio materials for using this information as part of a stress reduction program. The monitoring device is called the emWave2, and it is capable of acting as a portable recording monitor with a built in display as well as connecting to a PC for real-time display of heart rhythms."
HeartWizard[i] Tool Type: Hardware (pulse wave sensor) and software Data Type: Individual (Physiological Data: HRV via pulse wave sensor) Potential Use: Physiological Outputs	"A health improvement solution on your PC or laptop! Collects and analyses Heart Rate Variability (HRV) Data. An easy to use tool that gives you information about: —Mental and physical health—Mental and physical stress—Biological age—fitness & recovery level. Can be used to track your lifestyles changes."
meQuilibrium[j] Tool Type: Online service (platform) Data Type: Individual (diary with self-report on stressors) Potential Use: Psychological Outputs	"This is a web app to manage your stress. meQuilibrium is an individualized online environment, designed to teach you how to use your own personal thinking processes to your advantage. Every time you log in, you'll discover more about how your mind operates under the various kinds of stress that crop up in life. You'll get your "meQ" score and analysis of how you can improve it using a personalized skill development system."

(continued)

Table 5 (continued)

Tool overview	Description (http://quantifiedself.com/guide/)
MindMetrics Tool Type: Software (mobile app) Data Type: Individual (task performance) Potential Use: Psychological Outputs	"This app provides researchers, scientists, and interested individuals with a toolbox of cognitive tasks that are easy to administer, modify, analyze, and export. The tasks included in the application can be used to measure your arousal level, memory capacity, and multitasking abilities. Customize the difficulty level of the task, the number of trials administered, and the layout of the stimuli presented. Get individual response times by case and export the data collected to a comma-delimited format."
StressEraser[k] Tool Type: Hardware (handheld device and pulse wave sensor) Data Type: Individual (Physiological data: HRV via pulse wave sensor) Potential Use: Physiological Output	"StressEraser is a portable biofeedback device designed to help reduce stress by synchronizing breathing with heartrate. The device is a standalone unit that doesn't connect to a computer, instead displaying heart rate variability on a graphical display on the device itself, and indicating when to breath using visual cues."
Stresswatch[l] Tool Type: Wearable device (wristwatch) Data Type: Individual (Physiological data: HRV) Potential Use: Physiological Outputs	"Stresswatch is a heart rate variability sensor mounted on a watch strap, designed to provide feedback on stress levels. The watch indicates stress levels using a color chart on the device itself, and can also communicate data to smartphones, and PCs from where it can be transferred over the internet to medical professionals for further analysis. Stresswatch is a prototype under development."
Excluded: AffectCheck (discontinued) Basis heart rate monitor watch (recalled due to safety issues[m]) Pepfly (discontinued) Rationalizer (discontinued)	

[a]http://www.analyzewords.com/index.php (07/16/2017)
[b]https://itunes.apple.com/at/app/stress-check-by-azumio-lite/id500590587?mt=8 (07/16/2017)
[c]https://itunes.apple.com/at/app/stress-doctor-by-azumio-stress/id439290204?mt=8 (07/16/2017)
[d]http://www.azumio.com/s/instantheartrate/index.html (07/16/2017)
[e]http://bodymonitor.de/ (07/16/2017)
[f]http://cataphora-digital-mirror.software.informer.com/ (07/16/2017)
[g]https://itunes.apple.com/at/app/gottafeeling/id393588721?mt=8 (07/16/2017)
[h]http://store.heartmath.com/emwave2?_ga=1.98213274.483922243.1472026699 (07/16/2017)
[i]http://www.heartwizard.com/ (07/16/2017)
[j]https://www.mequilibrium.com/ (07/16/2017)
[k]http://www.stressstop.com/products/product.php?pid=79 (07/16/2017)
[l]http://quantifiedself.com/guide/tools/361/Stresswatch (07/16/2017)
[m]https://www.businessinsider.de/intel-safety-recall-for-basis-smartwatch-2016-8?r=US&IR=T (07/16/2017)

References

Abe, M., Morinishi, Y., Maeda, A., Aoki, M., & Inagaki, H. (2009). A life log collector integrated with a remote-controller for enabling user centric services. *IEEE Transactions on Consumer Electronics, 55*(1), 295–302. https://doi.org/10.1109/TCE.2009.4814448

Aizawa, K. (2013). Multimedia FoodLog: Diverse applications from self-monitoring to social contributions. *ITE Transactions on Media Technology and Applications, 1*(3), 214–219. https://doi.org/10.3169/mta.1.214

Aizawa, K., Maruyama, Y., Li, H., & Morikawa, C. (2013). Food balance estimation by using personal dietary tendencies in a multimedia food log. *IEEE Transactions on Multimedia, 15*(8), 2176–2185. https://doi.org/10.1109/TMM.2013.2271474

Aizawa, K., & Ogawa, M. (2015). FoodLog: Multimedia tool for healthcare applications. *IEEE Multimedia, 22*(2), 4–8. https://doi.org/10.1109/MMUL.2015.39

Albayram, Y., & Khan, M. M. H. (2015). Evaluating the effectiveness of using hints for autobiographical authentication: A field study. In *Proceedings of the 11th symposium on usable privacy and security (SOUPS 2015)* (pp. 211–224).

Albert, M. V., Toledo, S., Shapiro, M., & Kording, K. (2012). Using mobile phones for activity recognition in Parkinson's patients. *Frontiers in Neurology, 3*, 158. https://doi.org/10.3389/fneur.2012.00158

Alidina, S., Rosenthal, M. B., Schneider, E. C., Singer, S. J., & Friedberg, M. W. (2014). Practice environments and job satisfaction in patient-centered medical homes. *Annals of Family Medicine, 12*(4), 331–337. https://doi.org/10.1370/afm.1662

Amin, M. B., Banos, O., Khan, W. A., Muhammad Bilal, H. S., Gong, J., Bui, D.-M., … Lee, S. (2016). On curating multimodal sensory data for health and wellness platforms. *Sensors, 16* (7), 980. https://doi.org/10.3390/s16070980

Amiot, C. E., Terry, D. J., Jimmieson, N. L., & Callan, V. J. (2006). A longitudinal investigation of coping processes during a merger: Implications for job satisfaction and organizational identification. *Journal of Management, 32*(4), 552–574. https://doi.org/10.1177/0149206306287542

Anderson, I., Maitland, J., Sherwood, S., Barkhuus, L., Chalmers, M., Hall, M., … Muller, H. (2007). Shakra: Tracking and sharing daily activity levels with unaugmented mobile phones. *Mobile Networks and Applications, 12*(2–3), 185–199. https://doi.org/10.1007/s11036-007-0011-7

Anguita, D., Ghio, A., Oneto, L., Parra, X., & Reyes-Ortiz, J. L. (2012). Human activity recognition on smartphones for mobile context awareness. In *Proceedings of the 26th conference on advances in neural information processing systems* (pp. 1–9).

Anjum, A., & Ilyas, M. U. (2013). Activity recognition using smartphone sensors. In IEEE (Ed.) *Proceedings of the 10th consumer communications and networking conference (CCNC)* (pp. 914–919). https://doi.org/10.1109/CCNC.2013.6488584

Banos, O., Bilal Amin, M., Ali Khan, W., Afzal, M., Hussain, M., Kang, B. H., & Lee, S. (2016). The mining minds digital health and wellness framework. *Biomedical Engineering Online, 15* (Suppl 1), 76. https://doi.org/10.1186/s12938-016-0179-9

Banos, O., Villalonga, C., Bang, J., Hur, T., Kang, D., Park, S., … Lee, S. (2016). Human behavior analysis by means of multimodal context mining. *Sensors, 16*(8), pii: E1264. https://doi.org/10.3390/s16081264

Bao, X., & Choudhury, R. R. (2010). MoVi: Mobile phone based video highlights via collaborative sensing. In S. Banerjee, S. Keshav, & A. Wolman (Eds.), *Proceedings of the 8th international conference on mobile systems, applications, and services (MobiSys 2010)* (pp. 357–370). https://doi.org/10.1145/1814433.1814468

Berchtold, M., Budde, M., Gordon, D., Schmidtke, H. R., & Beigl, M. (2010). ActiServ: Activity recognition service for mobile phones. In *Proceedings of the 14th IEEE international symposium on wearable computers (ISWC 2010)* (pp. 1–8). https://doi.org/10.1109/ISWC.2010.5665868

Berry, E., Hampshire, A., Rowe, J., Hodges, S., Kapur, N., Watson, P., . . . Owen, A. M. (2009). The neural basis of effective memory therapy in a patient with limbic encephalitis. *Journal of Neurology, Neurosurgery, and Psychiatry, 80*(11), 1202–1205. https://doi.org/10.1136/jnnp.2008.164251

Berry, E., Kapur, N., Williams, L., Hodges, S. E., Watson, P., Smyth, G., . . . Wood, K. (2007). The use of a wearable camera, SenseCam, as a pictorial diary to improve autobiographical memory in a patient with limbic encephalitis: A preliminary report. *Neuropsychological Rehabilitation, 17*(4–5), 582–601. https://doi.org/10.1080/09602010601029780

Bicocchi, N., Castelli, G., Mamei, M., Rosi, A., & Zambonelli, F. (2008). Supporting location-aware services for mobile users with the whereabouts diary. In *Proceedings of the 1st international conference on MOBILe wireless MiddleWARE, operating systems, and applications, MOBILWARE 2008.*

Biggs, A., Brough, P., & Barbour, J. P. (2014). Relationships of individual and organizational support with engagement: Examining various types of causality in a three-wave study. *Work and Stress, 28*(3), 236–254. https://doi.org/10.1080/02678373.2014.934316

Blum, M., Pentland, A., & Troster, G. (2006). InSense: Interest-based life logging. *IEEE Multimedia, 13*(4), 40–48. https://doi.org/10.1109/MMUL.2006.87

Bono, J. E., Glomb, T. M., Shen, W., Kim, E., & Koch, A. J. (2013). Building positive resources: Effects of positive events and positive reflection on work stress and health. *Academy of Management Journal, 56*(6), 1601–1627. https://doi.org/10.5465/amj.2011.0272

Bragard, I., Etienne, A.-M., Merckaert, I., Libert, Y., & Razavi, D. (2010). Efficacy of a communication and stress management training on medical residents' self-efficacy, stress to communicate and burnout A randomized controlled study. *Journal of Health Psychology, 15*(7), 1075–1081. https://doi.org/10.1177/1359105310361992

Bravo, M. J., Peiro, J. M., Rodriguez, I., & Whitely, W. T. (2003). Social antecedents of the role stress and career-enhancing strategies of newcomers to organizations: A longitudinal study. *Work and Stress, 17*(3), 195–217. https://doi.org/10.1080/02678370310001625658

Brennan, A., Chugh, J. S., & Kline, T. (2002). Traditional versus open office design: A longitudinal field study. *Environment and Behavior, 34*(3), 279–299. https://doi.org/10.1177/0013916502034003001

Brindley, R., Bateman, A., & Gracey, F. (2011). Exploration of use of SenseCam to support autobiographical memory retrieval within a cognitive-behavioural therapeutic intervention following acquired brain injury. *Memory, 19*(7), 745–757. https://doi.org/10.1080/09658211.2010.493893

Brough, P., Timms, C., Siu, O.-L., Kalliath, T., O'Driscoll, M. P., Sit, C. H. P., . . . Lu, C.-Q. (2013). Validation of the Job Demands-Resources model in cross-national samples: Cross-sectional and longitudinal predictions of psychological strain and work engagement. *Human Relations, 66*(10), 1311–1335. https://doi.org/10.1177/0018726712472915

Browne, G., Berry, E., Kapur, N., Hodges, S., Smyth, G., Watson, P., & Wood, K. (2011). SenseCam improves memory for recent events and quality of life in a patient with memory retrieval difficulties. *Memory, 19*(7), 713–722. https://doi.org/10.1080/09658211.2011.614622

Byrne, D., Doherty, A. R., Jones, G. J. F., Smeaton, A. F., Kumpulainen, S., & Järvelin, K. (2008). The SenseCam as a tool for task observation. In O. Abuelmaatti (Ed.), *Proceedings of the 22nd British HCI Group annual conference on people and computers: Culture, creativity, interaction* (pp. 19–22). Swinton: British Computer Society. https://doi.org/10.1145/1531826.1531832

Byrne, D., Doherty, A. R., Snoek, C. G. M., Jones, G. J. F., & Smeaton, A. F. (2010). Everyday concept detection in visual lifelogs: Validation, relationships and trends. *Multimedia Tools and Applications, 49*(1), 119–144. https://doi.org/10.1007/s11042-009-0403-8

Chahuara, P., Fleury, A., Portet, F., Vacher, M., Hunter, G., Kymäläinen, T., & Herrera-Acuña, R. (2016). On-line human activity recognition from audio and home automation sensors: Comparison of sequential and non-sequential models in realistic Smart Homes. *Journal of Ambient Intelligence and Smart Environments, 8*(4), 399–422. https://doi.org/10.3233/AIS-160386

Chen, J., Foster, C., Kerr, J., Marshall, S. J., Wang, L., Godbole, S., . . . Patterson, R. (2013). Using the SenseCam as an objective tool for evaluating eating patterns. In J. Kerr, N. Weibel, & C. Gurrin (Eds.), *Proceedings of the 4th international SenseCam & pervasive imaging conference* (pp. 34–41). https://doi.org/10.1145/2526667.2526673

Chen, Y., & Jones, G. J. F. (2010). Augmenting human memory using personal lifelogs. In H. Saito, J.- M. Seigneur, G. Moreau, & P. Mistry (Eds.), *Proceedings of the 1st augmented human international conference* (pp. 1–9). https://doi.org/10.1145/1785455.1785479

Chen, Y., Jones, G. J. F., & Debasis, G. (2011). Segmenting and summarizing general events in a long-term lifelog. In *Proceedings of the 2nd workshop information access for personal media archives (IAPMA).*

Childs, J. H., & Stoeber, J. (2012). Do you want me to be perfect? Two longitudinal studies on socially prescribed perfectionism, stress and burnout in the workplace. *Work and Stress, 26*(4), 347–364. https://doi.org/10.1080/02678373.2012.737547

Cho, S.-B. (2016). Exploiting machine learning techniques for location recognition and prediction with smartphone logs. *Neurocomputing, 176*, 98–106. https://doi.org/10.1016/j.neucom.2015.02.079

Cho, S.-B., Kim, K. J., Hwang, K. S., & Song, I.-J. (2007). AniDiary: Daily cartoon-style diary exploits Bayesian networks. *IEEE Pervasive Computing, 6*(3), 66–75. https://doi.org/10.1109/MPRV.2007.49

Choi, W. -H., Kim, S. -I., Keum, M. -S., Han, W., Ko, H., & Han, D. K. (2011). Acoustic and visual signal based context awareness system for mobile application. In *IEEE international conference on consumer electronics (ICCE)* (pp. 627–628). Piscataway, NJ: IEEE. https://doi.org/10.1109/ICCE.2011.5722777

Choudhury, T., Borriello, G., Consolvo, S., Haehnel, D., Harrison, B., Hemingway, B., . . . Wyatt, D. (2008). The mobile sensing platform: An embedded activity recognition system. *IEEE Pervasive Computing, 7*(2), 32–41. https://doi.org/10.1109/MPRV.2008.39

Chowdhury, S., McParlane, P. J., Ferdous, M. S., & Jose, J. (2015). "My day in review": Visually summarising noisy lifelog data. In A. Hauptmann, C. -W. Ngo, X. Xue, Y. -G. Jiang, C. Snoek, & N. Vasconcelos (Eds.), *Proceedings of the 5th ACM on international conference on multimedia retrieval* (pp. 607–610). https://doi.org/10.1145/2671188.2749393

Connor, S. O., McCaffrey, N., Whyte, E., & Moran, K. (2016). The novel use of a SenseCam and accelerometer to validate training load and training information in a self-recall training diary. *Journal of Sports Sciences, 34*(4), 303–310 https://doi.org/10.1080/02640414.2015.1050600

Croon, E. M. de, Sluiter, J. K., Blonk, R. W., Broersen, J. P., & Frings-Dresen, M. H. (2004). Stressful work, psychological job strain, and turnover: A 2-year prospective cohort study of truck drivers. *Journal of Applied Psychology, 89*(3), 442–454. https://doi.org/10.1037/0021-9010.89.3.442

Derawi, M., & Bours, P. (2013). Gait and activity recognition using commercial phones. *Computers & Security, 39*, 137–144. https://doi.org/10.1016/j.cose.2013.07.004

Diestel, S., & Schmidt, K.-H. (2011). The moderating role of cognitive control deficits in the link from emotional dissonance to burnout symptoms and absenteeism. *Journal of Occupational Health Psychology, 16*(3), 313–330. https://doi.org/10.1037/a0022934

Dobbins, C., Merabti, M., Fergus, P., & Llewellyn-Jones, D. (2012). Augmenting human digital memories with physiological data. In IEEE (Ed.), *Proceedings of the 3rd IEEE international conference on networked embedded systems for every application* (pp. 1–7). https://doi.org/10.1109/NESEA.2012.6474032

Dobbins, C., Merabti, M., Fergus, P., & Llewellyn-Jones, D. (2014). Creating human digital memories with the aid of pervasive mobile devices. *Pervasive and Mobile Computing, 12*, 160–178. https://doi.org/10.1016/j.pmcj.2013.10.009

Doherty, A. R., Caprani, N., Conaire, C. Ó., Kalnikaite, V., Gurrin, C., Smeaton, A. F., & O'Connor, N. E. (2011). Passively recognising human activities through lifelogging. *Computers in Human Behavior, 27*(5), 1948–1958. https://doi.org/10.1016/j.chb.2011.05.002

Doherty, A. R., Kelly, P., Kerr, J., Marshall, S., Oliver, M., Badland, H., ... Foster, C. (2013). Using wearable cameras to categorise type and context of accelerometer-identified episodes of physical activity. *The International Journal of Behavioral Nutrition and Physical Activity, 10*, 22. https://doi.org/10.1186/1479-5868-10-22

Doherty, A. R., Moulin, C. J. A., & Smeaton, A. F. (2011). Automatically assisting human memory: A SenseCam browser. *Memory, 19*(7), 785–795. https://doi.org/10.1080/09658211.2010.509732

Doherty, A. R., Ó Conaire, C., Blighe, M., Smeaton, A. F., & O'Connor, N. E. (2008). Combining image descriptors to effectively retrieve events from visual lifelogs. In M. S. Lew, A. del Bimbo, & E. M. Bakker (Eds.), *Proceedings of the 1st ACM international conference on multimedia information retrieval* (pp. 10–17). https://doi.org/10.1145/1460096.1460100

Doherty, A. R., Pauly-Takacs, K., Caprani, N., Gurrin, C., Moulin, C. J. A., O'Connor, N. E., & Smeaton, A. F. (2012). Experiences of aiding autobiographical memory using the SenseCam. *Human-Computer Interaction, 27*, 151–174. https://doi.org/10.1080/07370024.2012.656050

Doherty, A. R., & Smeaton, A. F. (2010). Automatically augmenting lifelog events using pervasively generated content from millions of people. *Sensors, 10*(3), 1423–1446. https://doi.org/10.3390/s100301423

Edwards, J. A., Guppy, A., & Cockerton, T. (2007). A longitudinal study exploring the relationships between occupational stressors, non-work stressors, and work performance. *Work and Stress, 21*(2), 99–116. https://doi.org/10.1080/02678370701466900

Ellis, K., Kerr, J., Godbole, S., Staudenmayer, J., & Lanckriet, G. (2016). Hip and wrist accelerometer algorithms for free-living behavior classification. *Medicine and Science in Sports and Exercise, 48*(5), 933–940. https://doi.org/10.1249/MSS.0000000000000840

Elo, A.-L., & Ervasti, J. (2008). Evaluation of an organizational stress management program in a municipal public works organization. *Journal of Occupational Health Psychology, 13*(1), 10–23. https://doi.org/10.1037/1076-8998.13.1.10

Elovainio, M., Heponiemi, T., Jokela, M., Hakulinen, C., Presseau, J., Aalto, A.-M., & Kivimaeki, M. (2015). Stressful work environment and wellbeing: What comes first? *Journal of Occupational Health Psychology, 20*(3), 289–300. https://doi.org/10.1037/a0038684

Faye, S., Louveton, N., Gheorghe, G., & Engel, T. (2016). A two-level approach to characterizing human activities from wearable sensor data. *Journal of Wireless Mobile Networks, Ubiquitous Computing, and Dependable Applications, 7*(3), 1–21.

Fida, B., Bernabucci, I., Bibbo, D., Conforto, S., & Schmid, M. (2015). Varying behavior of different window sizes on the classification of static and dynamic physical activities from a single accelerometer. *Medical Engineering & Physics, 37*(7), 705–711. https://doi.org/10.1016/j.medengphy.2015.04.005

Finne, L. B., Knardahl, S., & Lau, B. (2011). Workplace bullying and mental distress: A prospective study of Norwegian employees. *Scandinavian Journal of Work Environment and Health, 37*(4), 276–287. https://doi.org/10.5271/sjweh.3156

Fugate, M., Kinicki, A. J., & Prussia, G. E. (2008). Employee coping with organizational change: An examination of alternative theoretical perspectives and models. *Personnel Psychology, 61*(1), 1–36. https://doi.org/10.1111/j.1744-6570.2008.00104.x

Fugate, M., Kinicki, A. J., & Scheck, C. L. (2002). Coping with an organizational merger over four stages. *Personnel Psychology, 55*(4), 905–928. https://doi.org/10.1111/j.1744-6570.2002.tb00134.x

Galais, N., & Moser, K. (2009). Organizational commitment and the well-being of temporary agency workers: A longitudinal study. *Human Relations, 62*(4), 589–620. https://doi.org/10.1177/0018726708101991

Ganti, R. K., Srinivasan, S., & Gacic, A. (2010). Multisensor fusion in smartphones for lifestyle monitoring. In *Proceedings of the 2010 international conference on body sensor networks (BSN)* (pp. 36–43). https://doi.org/10.1109/BSN.2010.10

Gemmell, J., Bell, G., & Lueder, R. (2006). MyLifeBits: A personal database for everything. *Communications of the ACM, 49*(1), 88–95. https://doi.org/10.1145/1107458.1107460

Gemming, L., Doherty, A., Kelly, P., Utter, J., & Ni Mhurchu, C. (2013). Feasibility of a SenseCam-assisted 24-h recall to reduce under-reporting of energy intake. *European Journal of Clinical Nutrition, 67*(10), 1095–1099. https://doi.org/10.1038/ejcn.2013.156

Gemming, L., Doherty, A., Utter, J., Shields, E., & Ni Mhurchu, C. (2015). The use of a wearable camera to capture and categorise the environmental and social context of self-identified eating episodes. *Appetite, 92*, 118–125. https://doi.org/10.1016/j.appet.2015.05.019

Gouveia, R., & Karapanos, E. (2013). Footprint tracker: Supporting diary studies with lifelogging. In W. E. Mackay, S. Brewster, & S. Bødker (Eds.), *Proceedings of the SIGCHI conference on human factors in computing systems* (pp. 2921–2930). https://doi.org/10.1145/2470654.2481405

Grau-Alberola, E., Gil-Monte, P. R., Garcia-Juesas, A. J., & Figueiredo-Ferraz, H. (2010). Incidence of burnout in Spanish nursing professionals: A longitudinal study. *International Journal of Nursing Studies, 47*(8), 1013–1020. https://doi.org/10.1016/j.ijnurstu.2009.12.022

Güldenpfennig, F., & Fitzpatrick, G. (2015). Personal digital archives on mobile phones with MEO. *Personal and Ubiquitous Computing, 19*(2), 445–461. https://doi.org/10.1007/s00779-014-0802-3

Gurrin, C., Qiu, Z., Hughes, M., Caprani, N., Doherty, A. R., Hodges, S. E., & Smeaton, A. F. (2013). The smartphone as a platform for wearable cameras in health research. *American Journal of Preventive Medicine, 44*(3), 308–313. https://doi.org/10.1016/j.amepre.2012.11.010

Gyorbiro, N., Fabian, A., & Hományi, G. (2009). An activity recognition system for mobile phones. *Mobile Networks and Applications, 14*(1), 82–91. https://doi.org/10.1007/s11036-008-0112-y

Han, M., Bang, J. H., Nugent, C., McClean, S., & Lee, S. (2014). A lightweight hierarchical activity recognition framework using smartphone sensors. *Sensors, 14*(9), 16181–16195. https://doi.org/10.3390/s140916181

Hanson, L. L. M., Chungkham, H. S., Akerstedt, T., & Westerlund, H. (2014). The role of sleep disturbances in the longitudinal relationship between psychosocial working conditions, measured by work demands and support, and depression. *Sleep, 37*(12), 1977–U139. https://doi.org/10.5665/sleep.4254

Hansson, A.-S., Vingard, E., Arnetz, B. B., & Anderzen, I. (2008). Organizational change, health, and sick leave among health care employees: A longitudinal study measuring stress markers, individual, and work site factors. *Work and Stress, 22*(1), 69–80. https://doi.org/10.1080/02678370801996236

Harper, R., Randall, D., Smyth, N., Evans, C., Heledd, L., & Moore, R. (2008). The past is a different place: They do things differently there. In J. van der Schijff & G. Marsden (Eds.), *Proceedings of the 7th ACM conference on designing interactive systems* (pp. 271–280). https://doi.org/10.1145/1394445.1394474

Hodges, S., Berry, E., & Wood, K. (2011). SenseCam: A wearable camera that stimulates and rehabilitates autobiographical memory. *Memory, 19*(7), 685–696. https://doi.org/10.1080/09658211.2011.605591

Hoobler, J. M., Rospenda, K. M., Lemmon, G., & Rosa, J. A. (2010). A within-subject longitudinal study of the effects of positive job experiences and generalized workplace harassment on well-being. *Journal of Occupational Health Psychology, 15*(4), 434–451. https://doi.org/10.1037/a0021000

Hou, B., Ogata, H., Li, M., & Uosaki, N. (2012). PACALL: Supporting language learning using SenseCam. In *Proceedings of the seventh IEEE international conference on wireless, mobile and ubiquitous technology in education* (pp. 331–332). https://doi.org/10.1109/WMUTE.2012.79

Hu, F., Smeaton, A. F., & Newman, E. (2014). Periodicity detection in lifelog data with missing and irregularly sampled data. In IEEE (Ed.), *Proceedings of BIBM 2014* (pp. 16–23). https://doi.org/10.1109/BIBM.2014.6999284

Huang, F.-M., Huang, Y. H., Szu, C., Su, A. Y., Chen, M. C., & Sun, Y. S. (2015). A study of a life logging smartphone app and its power consumption observation in location-based service scenario. In *Proceedings of the 2015 I.E. international conference on mobile services (MS)* (pp. 225–232). https://doi.org/10.1109/MobServ.2015.40

Hur, T., Bang, J., Kim, D., Banos, O., & Lee, S. (2017). Smartphone location-independent physical activity recognition based on transportation natural vibration analysis. *Sensors, 17*(4), pii: E931. https://doi.org/10.3390/s17040931

Hussain, S., Bang, J. H., Han, M., Ahmed, M. I., Amin, M. B., Lee, S., . . . Parr, G. (2014). Behavior life style analysis for mobile sensory data in cloud computing through MapReduce. *Sensors, 14* (11), 22001–22020. https://doi.org/10.3390/s141122001

Hwang, K.-S., & Cho, S.-B. (2009). Landmark detection from mobile life log using a modular bayesian network model. *Expert Systems with Applications, 36*(10), 12065–12076. https://doi.org/10.1016/j.eswa.2009.03.002

Hyvonen, K., Feldt, T., Kinnunen, U., & Tolvanen, A. (2011). Changes in personal work goals in relation to the psychosocial work environment: A two-year follow-up study. *Work and Stress, 25*(4), 289–308. https://doi.org/10.1080/02678373.2012.630587

Idris, M. A., Dollard, M. F., & Yulita. (2014). Psychosocial safety climate, emotional demands, burnout, and depression: A longitudinal multilevel study in the Malaysian private sector. *Journal of Occupational Health Psychology, 19*(3), 291–302. https://doi.org/10.1037/a0036599

Ilies, R., Schwind, K. M., Wagner, D. T., & Johnson, M. D. (2007). When can employees have a family life ? the effects of daily workload and affect on work-family conflict and social Behaviors at home. *Journal of Applied Psychology, 92*(5), 1368–1379. https://doi.org/10.1037/0021-9010.92.5.1368

Isaacs, E., Konrad, A., Walendowski, A., Lennig, T., Hollis, V., & Whittaker, S. (2013). Echoes from the past: How technology mediated reflection improves well-being. In W. E. Mackay, S. Brewster, & S. Bødker (Eds.), *Proceedings of the SIGCHI conference on human factors in computing systems* (p. 1071). https://doi.org/10.1145/2470654.2466137

Ivonin, L., Chang, H.-M., Chen, W., & Rauterberg, M. (2013). Unconscious emotions: Quantifying and logging something we are not aware of. *Personal and Ubiquitous Computing, 17*(4), 663–673. https://doi.org/10.1007/s00779-012-0514-5

Jacques, P. L. S., Conway, M. A., & Cabeza, R. (2011). Gender differences in autobiographical memory for everyday events: Retrieval elicited by SenseCam images versus verbal cues. *Memory, 19*(7), 723–732. https://doi.org/10.1080/09658211.2010.516266

Jacques, P. L. S., Conway, M. A., Lowder, M. W., & Cabeza, R. (2011). Watching my mind unfold versus yours: An fMRI study using a novel camera technology to examine neural differences in self-projection of self versus other perspectives. *Journal of Cognitive Neuroscience, 23*(6), 1275–1284.

Jalali, L., & Jain, R. (2013). Building health persona from personal data streams. In V. K. Singh, T. -S. Chua, R. Jain, & A. S. Pentland (Eds.), *Proceedings of the 1st ACM international workshop on personal data meets distributed multimedia* (pp. 19–26). https://doi.org/10.1145/2509352.2509400

Jeon, J. H., Yeon, J., Lee, S.-G., & Seo, J. (2014). Exploratory visualization of smartphone-based life-logging data using smart reality testbed. In IEEE (Ed.), *2014 international conference on big data and smart computing (BIGCOMP)* (pp. 29–33). https://doi.org/10.1109/BIGCOMP.2014.6741400

Jimmieson, N. L., Terry, D. J., & Callan, V. J. (2004). A longitudinal study of employee adaptation to organizational change: The role of change-related information and change-related self-efficacy. *Journal of Occupational Health Psychology, 9*(1), 11–27. https://doi.org/10.1037/1076-8998.9.1.11

Kalnikaite, V., & Whittaker, S. (2011). A saunter down memory lane: Digital reflection on personal mementos. *International Journal of Human-Computer Studies, 69*(5), 298–310.

Kang, B., Moudon, A. V., Hurvitz, P. M., Reichley, L., & Saelens, B. E. (2013). Walking objectively measured: Classifying accelerometer data with GPS and travel diaries. *Medicine and Science in Sports and Exercise, 45*(7), 1419–1428.

Kawamura, T., Fukuhara, T., Takeda, H., Kono, Y., & Kidode, M. (2007). Ubiquitous memories: A memory externalization system using physical objects. *Personal and Ubiquitous Computing, 11* (4), 287–298. https://doi.org/10.1007/s00779-006-0085-4

Kelly, L., & Jones, G. J. F. (2009). Examining the utility of affective response in search of personal lifelogs. In *Proceedings of the 5th workshop on emotion in human-computer interaction.*

Kelly, P., Doherty, A., Mizdrak, A., Marshall, S., Kerr, J., Legge, A., … Foster, C. (2014). High group level validity but high random error of a self-report travel diary, as assessed by wearable cameras. *Journal of Transport & Health, 1*(3), 190–201. https://doi.org/10.1016/j.jth.2014.04.003

Kelly, P., Doherty, A. R., Berry, E., Hodges, S. E., Batterham, A. M., & Foster, C. (2011). Can we use digital life-log images to investigate active and sedentary travel behaviour? Results from a pilot study. *The International Journal of Behavioral Nutrition and Physical Activity, 8*, 44. https://doi.org/10.1186/1479-5868-8-44

Kelly, P., Thomas, E., Doherty, A., Harms, T., Burke, O., Gershuny, J., & Foster, C. (2015). Developing a method to test the validity of 24 hour time use diaries using wearable cameras: A feasibility pilot. *PLoS ONE, 10*(12), e0142198. https://doi.org/10.1371/journal.pone.0142198

Kern, N., Schiele, B., & Schmidt, A. (2007). Recognizing context for annotating a live life recording. *Personal and Ubiquitous Computing, 11*(4), 251–263. https://doi.org/10.1007/s00779-006-0086-3

Kerr, J., Marshall, S. J., Godbole, S., Chen, J., Legge, A., Doherty, A. R., … Foster, C. (2013). Using the SenseCam to improve classifications of sedentary behavior in free-living settings. *American Journal of Preventive Medicine, 44*(3), 290–296. https://doi.org/10.1016/j.amepre.2012.11.004

Khan, A. M., Siddiqi, M. H., & Lee, S.-W. (2013). Exploratory data analysis of acceleration signals to select light-weight and accurate features for real-time activity recognition on smartphones. *Sensors, 13*(10), 13099–13122. https://doi.org/10.3390/s131013099

Kikhia, B., Boytsov, A., Hallberg, J., ul Hussain Sani, Z., Jonsson, H., & Synnes, K. (2014). Structuring and presenting lifelogs based on location data. In P. Cipresso, A. Matic, & G. Lopez (Eds.), *Lecture notes of the Institute for Computer Sciences, Social Informatics and Telecommunications Engineering. Pervasive computing paradigms for mental health. Proceedings of the 4th international symposium, MindCare 2014* (Vol. 100, pp. 133–144). Cham: Springer. https://doi.org/10.1007/978-3-319-11564-1_14

Kikhia, B., Hallberg, J., Bengtsson, J. E., Savenstedt, S., & Synnes, K. (2010). Building digital life stories for memory support. *International Journal of Computers in Healthcare, 1*(2), 161–176. https://doi.org/10.1504/IJCIH.2010.037460

Kim, M., Lee, D.-W., Kim, K., & Kim, J.-H. (2015). Hierarchical structured data logging system for effective lifelog management in ubiquitous environment. *Multimedia Tools and Applications, 74*(10), 3561–3577. https://doi.org/10.1007/s11042-013-1671-x

Korunka, C., Scharitzer, D., Carayon, P., & Sainfort, F. (2003). Employee strain and job satisfaction related to an implementation of quality in a public service organization: A longitudinal study. *Work and Stress, 17*(1), 52–72. https://doi.org/10.1080/0267837031000109526

Kumar, G., Jerbi, H., Gurrin, C., & O'Mahony, M. P. (2014). Towards activity recommendation from lifelogs. In M. Indrawan-Santiago, M. Steinbauer, H. -Q. Nguyen, A. M. Tjoa, I. Khalil, & G. Anderst-Kotsis (Eds.), *Proceedings of the 16th international conference on information integration and web-based applications & services* (pp. 87–96). https://doi.org/10.1145/2684200.2684298

Kwapisz, J. R., Weiss, G. M., & Moore, S. A. (2010). Activity recognition using cell phone accelerometers. *ACM SIGKDD Explorations Newsletter, 12*(2), 74–92. https://doi.org/10.1145/1964897.1964918

Lang, J., Bliese, P. D., Lang, J. W. B., & Adler, A. B. (2011). Work gets unfair for the depressed: Cross-lagged relations between organizational justice perceptions and depressive symptoms. *Journal of Applied Psychology, 96*(3), 602–618. https://doi.org/10.1037/a0022463

Lee, H., Smeaton, A. F., O'Connor, N. E., Jones, G., Blighe, M., Byrne, D., ... Gurrin, C. (2008). Constructing a SenseCam visual diary as a media process. *Multimedia Systems, 14*(6), 341–349.

Lee, M.-W., Khan, A. M., & Kim, T.-S. (2011). A single tri-axial accelerometer-based real-time personal life log system capable of human activity recognition and exercise information generation. *Personal and Ubiquitous Computing, 15*(8), 887–898. https://doi.org/10.1007/s00779-011-0403-3

Lee, Y. -S., & Cho, S. -B. (2011a). Activity recognition using hierarchical hidden Markov models on a smartphone with 3D accelerometer. In D. Hutchison, T. Kanade, J. Kittler, J. M. Kleinberg, F. Mattern, J. C. Mitchell, ... M. Woźniak (Eds.), *Lecture notes in computer science. Proceedings of the 6th international conference on hybrid artificial intelligent systems* (Vol. 6678, pp. 460–467). Berlin: Springer. https://doi.org/10.1007/978-3-642-21219-2_58

Lee, Y.-S., & Cho, S.-B. (2011b). Exploiting mobile contexts for Petri-net to generate a story in cartoons. *Applied Intelligence, 34*(1), 1–18. https://doi.org/10.1007/s10489-009-0175-x

Lee, Y.-S., & Cho, S.-B. (2013). Mobile context inference using two-layered Bayesian networks for smartphones. *Expert Systems with Applications, 40*(11), 4333–4345. https://doi.org/10.1016/j.eswa.2013.01.018

Lee, Y.-S., & Cho, S.-B. (2014). Activity recognition with android phone using mixture-of-experts co-trained with labeled and unlabeled data. *Neurocomputing, 126*, 106–115. https://doi.org/10.1016/j.neucom.2013.05.044

Lee, Y.-S., & Cho, S.-B. (2016). Layered hidden Markov models to recognize activity with built-in sensors on Android smartphone. *Pattern Analysis and Applications, 19*(4), 1181–1193 https://doi.org/10.1007/s10044-016-0549-8

Li, N., Crane, M., Gurrin, C., & Ruskin, H. J. (2016). Finding motifs in large personal lifelogs. In A. Schmidt, T. Terada, W. Woo, P. Mistry, J. -M. Seigneur, J. M. Hernandez-Munoz, & P. McCullagh (Eds.), *Proceedings of the 7th augmented human international conference* (pp. 1–8). https://doi.org/10.1145/2875194.2875214

Lim, S., Lee, S.-H., & Cho, S.-B. (2016). A modular approach to landmark detection based on a Bayesian network and categorized context logs. *Information Sciences, 330*, 145–156. https://doi.org/10.1016/j.ins.2015.10.017

Lindley, S. E., Glancy, M., Harper, R., Randall, D., & Smyth, N. (2011). "Oh and how things just don't change, the more things stay the same": Reflections on SenseCam images 18 months after capture. *International Journal of Human-Computer Studies, 69*(5), 311–323. https://doi.org/10.1016/j.ijhcs.2010.12.010

Lockhart, J. W., & Weiss, G. M. (2014). The benefits of personalized smartphone-based activity recognition models. In M. Zaki, Z. Obradovic, P. N. Tan, A. Banerjee, C. Kamath, & S. Parthasarathy (Eds.), *Proceedings of the 2014 SIAM international conference on data mining* (pp. 614–622). Philadelphia, PA: Society for Industrial and Applied Mathematics. https://doi.org/10.1137/1.9781611973440.71

Loveday, C., & Conway, M. A. (2011). Using SenseCam with an amnesic patient: Accessing inaccessible everyday memories. *Memory, 19*(7), 697–704. https://doi.org/10.1080/09658211.2011.610803

Mafrur, R., Nugraha, I. G. D., & Choi, D. (2015). Modeling and discovering human behavior from smartphone sensing life-log data for identification purpose. *Human-centric Computing and Information Sciences, 5*(1), 17. https://doi.org/10.1186/s13673-015-0049-7

Marinac, C., Merchant, G., Godbole, S., Chen, J., Kerr, J., Clark, B., & Marshall, S. (2013). The feasibility of using SenseCams to measure the type and context of daily sedentary behaviors. In J. Kerr, N. Weibel, & C. Gurrin (Eds.), *Proceedings of the 4th international SenseCam & pervasive imaging conference* (pp. 42–49). https://doi.org/10.1145/2526667.2526674

Martín, H., Bernardos, A. M., Iglesias, J., & Casar, J. R. (2013). Activity logging using lightweight classification techniques in mobile devices. *Personal and Ubiquitous Computing, 17*(4), 675–695. https://doi.org/10.1007/s00779-012-0515-4

Maslach, C., & Leiter, M. P. (2008). Early predictors of job burnout and engagement. *Journal of Applied Psychology, 93*(3), 498–512. https://doi.org/10.1037/0021-9010.93.3.498

Merler, M., Wu, H., Uceda-Sosa, R., Nguyen, Q.-B., & Smith, J. R. (2016). Snap, Eat, RepEat: A food recognition engine for dietary logging. In S. Mougiakakou, G. M. Farinella, & K. Yanai (Eds.), *Proceedings of the 2nd international workshop on multimedia assisted dietary management* (pp. 31–40). https://doi.org/10.1145/2986035.2986036

Miluzzo, E., Lane, N. D., Fodor, K., Peterson, R., Lu, H., Musolesi, M., . . . Campbell, A. T. (2008). Sensing meets mobile social networks. In T. Abdelzaher, M. Martonosi, & A. Wolisz (Eds.), *Proceedings of the 6th ACM conference on embedded network sensor systems* (pp. 337–350). https://doi.org/10.1145/1460412.1460445

Moen, P., Kelly, E. L., Fan, W., Lee, S.-R., Almeida, D., Kossek, E. E., & Buxton, O. M. (2016). Does a flexibility/support organizational initiative improve high-tech employees' well-being? Evidence from the work, family, and health network. *American Sociological Review, 81*(1), 134–164. https://doi.org/10.1177/0003122415622391

Moen, P., Kelly, E. L., & Lam, J. (2013). Healthy work revisited: Do changes in time strain predict well-being? *Journal of Occupational Health Psychology, 18*(2), 157–172. https://doi.org/10.1037/a0031804

Moghimi, M., Wu, W., Chen, J., Godbole, S., Marshall, S., Kerr, J., & Belongie, S. (2014). Analyzing sedentary behavior in life-logging images. In IEEE (Ed.), *Proceedings of the international conference on image processing (ICIP)* (pp. 1011–1015). https://doi.org/10.1109/ICIP.2014.7025202

Mortazavi, B., Nemati, E., VanderWall, K., Flores-Rodriguez, H. G., Cai, J. Y. J., Lucier, J., . . . Sarrafzadeh, M. (2015). Can smartwatches replace smartphones for posture tracking? *Sensors, 15*(10), 26783–26800. https://doi.org/10.3390/s151026783

Moyle, P. (1998). Longitudinal influences of managerial support on employee well-being. *Work and Stress, 12*(1), 29–49. https://doi.org/10.1080/02678379808256847

Murphy, F. C., Barnard, P. J., Terry, K. A. M., Carthery-Goulart, M. T., & Holmes, E. A. (2011). SenseCam, imagery and bias in memory for wellbeing. *Memory, 19*(7), 768–777. https://doi.org/10.1080/09658211.2010.551130

Naeswall, K., Sverke, M., & Goeransson, S. (2014). Is work affecting my health? Appraisals of how work affects health as a mediator in the relationship between working conditions and work-related attitudes. *Work and Stress, 28*(4), 342–361. https://doi.org/10.1080/02678373.2014.959092

Nam, Y., Rho, S., & Lee, C. (2013). Physical activity recognition using multiple sensors embedded in a wearable device. *ACM Transactions on Embedded Computing Systems, 12*(2), 1–14. https://doi.org/10.1145/2423636.2423644

Nielsen, K., & Randall, R. (2012). The importance of employee participation and perceptions of changes in procedures in a teamworking intervention. *Work and Stress, 26*(2), 91–111. https://doi.org/10.1080/02678373.2012.682721

Nielsen, K., Randall, R., & Albertsen, K. (2007). Participants' appraisals of process issues and the effects of stress management interventions. *Journal of Organizational Behavior, 28*(6), 793–810. https://doi.org/10.1002/job.450

Nielsen, M. B., Hetland, J., Matthiesen, S. B., & Einarsen, S. (2012). Longitudinal relationships between workplace bullying and psychological distress. *Scandinavian Journal of Work Environment and Health, 38*(1), 38–46. https://doi.org/10.5271/sjweh.3178

Nishiyama, Y., Okoshi, T., Yonezawa, T., Nakazawa, J., Takashio, K., & Tokuda, H. (2016). Towards health exercise behavior change for teams using lifelog sharing models. *IEEE Journal of Biomedical and Health Informatics, 20*(3), 775–786. https://doi.org/10.1109/JBHI.2015.2478903

Odle-Dusseau, H. N., Herleman, H. L. A., Britt, T. W., Moore, D. D., Castro, C. A., & McGurk, D. (2013). Family-supportive work environments and psychological strain: A longitudinal test of two theories. *Journal of Occupational Health Psychology, 18*(1), 27–36. https://doi.org/10.1037/a0030803

Ogata, H., Hou, B., Li, M., Uosaki, N., Mouri, K., & Liu, S. (2014). Ubiquitous learning project using life-logging technology in Japan. *Educational Technology & Society, 17*(2), 85–100.

Ogata, H., Li, M., Hou, B., Uosaki, N., El-Bishouty, M. M., & Yano, Y. (2011). SCROLL: Supporting to share and reuse ubiquitous learning log in the context of language learning. *Research and Practice in Technology Enhanced Learning, 6*(2), 69–82.

Ogata, H., Misumi, T., Matsuka, T., El-Bishouty, M. M., & Yano, Y. (2008). A framework for capturing, sharing and comparing learning experiences in a ubiquitous learning environment. *Research and Practice in Technology Enhanced Learning, 03*(03), 297–312.

Ohsawa, R., Takashio, K., & Tokuda, H. (2006). OreDesk: A tool for retrieving data history based on user operations. In IEEE (Ed.), *Proceedings of the 8th international symposium on multimedia (ISM 2006)* (pp. 762–765). https://doi.org/10.1109/ISM.2006.121

Okamoto, K., & Yanai, K. (2014, July 14–18). Real-time eating action recognition system on a smartphone. In *Proceedings of the IEEE international conference on multimedia and expo workshops, Chengdu, China* (pp. 1–6). https://doi.org/10.1109/ICMEW.2014.6890718

Oliver, M., Doherty, A. R., Kelly, P., Badland, H. M., Mavoa, S., Shepherd, J., ... Foster, C. (2013). Utility of passive photography to objectively audit built environment features of active transport journeys: An observational study. *International Journal of Health Geographics, 12*, 20. https://doi.org/10.1186/1476-072X-12-20

Otebolaku, A. M., & Andrade, M. T. (2013). Recognizing high-level contexts from smartphone built-In sensors for mobile media content recommendation. In IEEE (Ed.), *Proceedings of the 14th international conference on mobile data management (MDM)* (pp. 142–147). https://doi.org/10.1109/MDM.2013.84

Otebolaku, A. M., & Andrade, M. T. (2016). User context recognition using smartphone sensors and classification models. *Journal of Network and Computer Applications, 66*, 33–51. https://doi.org/10.1016/j.jnca.2016.03.013

Palumbo, F., Gallicchio, C., Pucci, R., & Micheli, A. (2016). Human activity recognition using multisensor data fusion based on Reservoir Computing. *Journal of Ambient Intelligence and Smart Environments, 8*(2), 87–107. https://doi.org/10.3233/AIS-160372

Park, H.-S., & Cho, S.-B. (2011). A personalized summarization of video life-logs from an indoor multi-camera system using a fuzzy rule-based system with domain knowledge. *Information Systems, 36*(8), 1124–1134. https://doi.org/10.1016/j.is.2011.04.005

Park, H.-S., Oh, K., & Cho, S.-B. (2011). Bayesian network-based high-level context recognition for mobile context sharing in cyber-physical system. *International Journal of Distributed Sensor Networks, 7*(1), 650387. https://doi.org/10.1155/2011/650387

Pas, E. T., Bradshaw, C. P., & Hershfeldt, P. A. (2012). Teacher- and school-level predictors of teacher efficacy and burnout: Identifying potential areas for support. *Journal of School Psychology, 50*(1), 129–145. https://doi.org/10.1016/j.jsp.2011.07.003

Pauly-Takacs, K., Moulin, C. J. A., & Estlin, E. J. (2011). SenseCam as a rehabilitation tool in a child with anterograde amnesia. *Memory, 19*(7), 705–712.

Pendergast, F. J., Ridgers, N. D., Worsley, A., & McNaughton, S. A. (2017). Evaluation of a smartphone food diary application using objectively measured energy expenditure. *The International Journal of Behavioral Nutrition and Physical Activity, 14*(1), 30. https://doi.org/10.1186/s12966-017-0488-9

Pernek, I., Stiglic, G., & Kokol, P. (2012). How hard am I training? Using smart phones to estimate sport activity intensity. In *Proceedings of the international conference on distributed computing systems workshops* (pp. 65–68). https://doi.org/10.1109/ICDCSW.2012.34

Petrou, P., Demerouti, E., & Schaufeli, W. B. (2015). Job crafting in changing organizations: Antecedents and implications for exhaustion and performance. *Journal of Occupational Health Psychology, 20*(4), 470–480. https://doi.org/10.1037/a0039003

Puangpakisiri, W., Yamasaki, T., & Aizawa, K. (2008). High level activity annotation of daily experiences by a combination of a wearable device and Wi-Fi based positioning system. In *Proceedings of the IEEE international conference on multimedia and expo* (pp. 1421–1424). https://doi.org/10.1109/ICME.2008.4607711

Qiu, Z., Doherty, A. R., Gurrin, C., & Smeaton, A. F. (2011). Mining user activity as a context source for search and retrieval. In *Proceedings of the international conference on semantic technology and information retrieval (STAIR)* (pp. 162–166). https://doi.org/10.1109/STAIR.2011.5995782

Rai, A., Yan, Z., Chakraborty, D., Wijaya, T. K., & Aberer, K. (2012). Mining complex activities in the wild via a single smartphone accelerometer. In D. Das, A. R. Ganguly, V. Chandola, O. A. Omitaomu, K. Steinhaeuser, J. Gama, ... N. V. Chawla (Eds.), *Proceedings of the sixth international workshop on knowledge discovery from sensor data* (pp. 43–51). https://doi.org/10.1145/2350182.2350187

Rawassizadeh, R., Momeni, E., Dobbins, C., Mirza-Babaei, P., & Rahnamoun, R. (2015). Lesson learned from collecting quantified self information via mobile and wearable devices. *Journal of Sensor and Actuator Networks, 4*(4), 315–335. https://doi.org/10.3390/jsan4040315

Rawassizadeh, R., Tomitsch, M., Nourizadeh, M., Momeni, E., Peery, A., Ulanova, L., & Pazzani, M. (2015). Energy-efficient integration of continuous context sensing and prediction into smartwatches. *Sensors, 15*(9), 22616–22645. https://doi.org/10.3390/s150922616

Rawassizadeh, R., Tomitsch, M., Wac, K., & Tjoa, A. M. (2013). UbiqLog: A generic mobile phone-based life-log framework. *Personal and Ubiquitous Computing, 17*(4), 621–637.

Reknes, I., Pallesen, S., Mageroy, N., Moen, B. E., Bjorvatn, B., & Einarsen, S. (2014). Exposure to bullying behaviors as a predictor of mental health problems among Norwegian nurses: Results from the prospective SUSSH-survey. *International Journal of Nursing Studies, 51*(3), 479–487. https://doi.org/10.1016/j.ijnurstu.2013.06.017

Riedl, R. (2013). On the biology of technostress: Literature review and research agenda. *Data Base for Advances in Information Systems, 44*(1), 18–55. https://doi.org/10.1145/2436239.2436242

Rizzuto, T. E., Mohammed, S., & Vance, R. J. (2011). Marching in-step: Facilitating technological transitions through climate consensus. *Computers in Human Behavior, 27*(1), 185–194. https://doi.org/10.1016/j.chb.2010.07.035

Ryoo, D.-W., & Bae, C. (2007). Design of the wearable gadgets for life-log services based on UTC. *IEEE Transactions on Consumer Electronics, 53*(4), 1477–1482. https://doi.org/10.1109/TCE.2007.4429240

Saeedi, S., & El-Sheimy, N. (2015). Activity recognition using fusion of low-cost sensors on a smartphone for mobile navigation application. *Micromachines, 6*(8), 1100–1134. https://doi.org/10.3390/mi6081100

Safadi, B., Mulhem, P., Quenot, G., & Chevallet, J. -P. (2016). Lifelog semantic annotation using deep visual features and metadata-derived descriptors. In IEEE (Ed.), *Proceedings of the 14th international workshop on content-based multimedia indexing (CBMI)* (pp. 1–6). https://doi.org/10.1109/CBMI.2016.7500247

Sanchez, J. I., & Viswesvaran, C. (2002). The effects of temporal separation on the relations between self-reported work stressors and strains. *Organizational Research Methods, 5*(2), 173–183. https://doi.org/10.1177/1094428102005002003

San-Segundo, R., Lorenzo-Trueba, J., Martínez-González, B., & Pardo, J. M. (2016). Segmenting human activities based on HMMs using smartphone inertial sensors. *Pervasive and Mobile Computing, 30*, 84–96. https://doi.org/10.1016/j.pmcj.2016.01.004

Sas, C., Fratczak, T., Rees, M., Gellersen, H., Kalnikaite, V., Coman, A., & Höök, K. (2013). AffectCam: Arousal-augmented SenseCam for richer recall of episodic memories. In W. E. Mackay, S. Brewster, & S. Bødker (Eds.), *CHI '13 extended abstracts on human factors in computing systems* (pp. 1041–1046). https://doi.org/10.1145/2468356.2468542

Shoaib, M., Bosch, S., Incel, O. D., Scholten, H., & Havinga, P. J. M. (2016). Complex human activity recognition using smartphone and wrist-worn motion sensors. *Sensors, 16*(4), 426. https://doi.org/10.3390/s16040426

Silva, G. C. de, Yamasaki, T., & Aizawa, K. (2007). An interactive multimedia diary for the home. *Computer, 40*(5), 52–59. https://doi.org/10.1109/MC.2007.155

Smith, A., O'Hara, K., & Lewis, P. (2011). Visualising the past: Annotating a life with linked open data. In D. de Roure & S. Poole (Eds.), *Proceedings of the 3rd international web science conference* (pp. 1–8). https://doi.org/10.1145/2527031.2527038

Smith, B. K., Frost, J., Albayrak, M., & Sudhakar, R. (2007). Integrating glucometers and digital photography as experience capture tools to enhance patient understanding and communication of diabetes self-management practices. *Personal and Ubiquitous Computing, 11*(4), 273–286. https://doi.org/10.1007/s00779-006-0087-2

Steptoe, A., Wardle, J., Lipsey, Z., Mills, R., Oliver, G., Jarvis, M., & Kirschbaum, C. (1998). A longitudinal study of work load and variations in psychological well-being, cortisol, smoking, and alcohol consumption. *Annals of Behavioral Medicine, 20*(2), 84–91. https://doi.org/10.1007/BF02884453

Stiglbauer, B., Selenko, E., Batinic, B., & Jodlbauer, S. (2012). On the link between job insecurity and turnover intentions: Moderated mediation by work involvement and well-being. *Journal of Occupational Health Psychology, 17*(3), 354–364. https://doi.org/10.1037/a0028565

Sun, L., Zhang, D., Li, B., Guo, B., & Li, S. (2010). Activity recognition on an accelerometer embedded mobile phone with varying positions and orientations. In D. Hutchison, T. Kanade, J. Kittler, J. M. Kleinberg, F. Mattern, J. C. Mitchell, ... X. Zhou (Eds.), *Lecture notes in computer science: Vol. 6406. Ubiquitous intelligence and computing* (Vol. 6406, pp. 548–562). Berlin: Springer. https://doi.org/10.1007/978-3-642-16355-5_42

Sun, L., Zhang, D., & Li, N. (2011). Physical activity monitoring with mobile phones. In D. Hutchison, T. Kanade, J. Kittler, J. M. Kleinberg, F. Mattern, J. C. Mitchell, ... M. Mokhtari (Eds.), *Lecture notes in computer science: Vol. 6719. Toward useful services for elderly and people with disabilities* (Vol. 6719, pp. 104–111). Berlin: Springer. https://doi.org/10.1007/978-3-642-21535-3_14

Teraoka, T. (2012). Organization and exploration of heterogeneous personal data collected in daily life. *Human-centric Computing and Information Sciences, 2*(1), 1. https://doi.org/10.1186/2192-1962-2-1

Terziyski, S., Albatal, R., & Gurrin, C. (2015). Fast human activity recognition in lifelogging. In X. He, S. Luo, D. Tao, C. Xu, J. Yang, & M. A. Hasan (Eds.), *Lecture notes in computer science: Vol. 8936. MultiMedia modeling* (Vol. 8936, pp. 369–379). Cham: Springer. https://doi.org/10.1016/j.patrec.2011.07.013

Torres-Huitzil, C., & Nuno-Maganda, M. (2015). Robust smartphone-based human activity recognition using a tri-axial accelerometer. In IEEE (Ed.), *Proceedings of the 6th Latin American symposium on circuits & systems (LASCAS 2015)* (pp. 1–4). https://doi.org/10.1109/LASCAS.2015.7250435

Tyson, P. D., & Pongruengphant, R. (2004). Five-year follow-up study of stress among nurses in public and private hospitals in Thailand. *International Journal of Nursing Studies, 41*(3), 247–254. https://doi.org/10.1016/S0020-7489(03)00134-2

Vander Elst, T., Richter, A., Sverke, M., Naeswall, K., Cuyper, N. de, & Witte, H. de. (2014). Threat of losing valued job features: The role of perceived control in mediating the effect of qualitative job insecurity on job strain and psychological withdrawal. Work and Stress, 28(2), 143–164. https://doi.org/10.1080/02678373.2014.899651

Vemuri, S., & Bender, W. (2004). Next-generation personal memory aids. *BT Technology Journal, 22*(4), 125–138. https://doi.org/10.1023/B:BTTJ.0000047591.29175.89

Vemuri, S., Schmandt, C., & Bender, W. (2006). iRemember: A personal, long-term memory prosthesis. In K. Mase (Ed.), *Proceedings of the 3rd ACM workshop on continuous archival and retrieval of personal experiences* (pp. 65–74). https://doi.org/10.1145/1178657.1178670

Wang, J., Patten, S. B., Currie, S., Sareen, J., & Schmitz, N. (2012). A population-based longitudinal study on work environmental factors and the risk of major depressive disorder. *American Journal of Epidemiology, 176*(1), 52–59. https://doi.org/10.1093/aje/kwr473

Wang, M., Zhan, Y., McCune, E., & Truxillo, D. (2011). Understanding newcomers' adaptability and work-related outcomes: Testing the mediating roles of perceived P-E Fit variables. *Personnel Psychology, 64*(1), 163–189. https://doi.org/10.1111/j.1744-6570.2010.01205.x

Wang, P., & Smeaton, A. F. (2011). Aggregating semantic concepts for event representation in lifelogging. In R. de Virgilio, F. Giunchiglia, & L. Tanca (Eds.), *Proceedings of the*

international workshop on semantic web information management (pp. 1–6). https://doi.org/10.1145/1999299.1999307
Wang, P., & Smeaton, A. F. (2012). Semantics-based selection of everyday concepts in visual lifelogging. *International Journal of Multimedia Information Retrieval, 1*(2), 87–101.
Wang, P., & Smeaton, A. F. (2013). Using visual lifelogs to automatically characterize everyday activities. *Information Sciences, 230*, 147–161. https://doi.org/10.1016/j.ins.2012.12.028
Wang, P., Smeaton, A. F., Zhang, Y. C., & Deng, B. (2014). Enhancing the detection of concepts for visual lifelogs using contexts instead of ontologies. In IEEE (Ed.), *Proceedings of ICMEW 2014* (pp. 1–6).
Wang, P., Sun, L., Yang, S., Smeaton, A. F., & Gurrin, C. (2016). Characterizing everyday activities from visual lifelogs based on enhancing concept representation. *Computer Vision and Image Understanding, 148*, 181–192. https://doi.org/10.1016/j.cviu.2015.09.014
Weiss, G. M., Timko, J. L., Gallagher, C. M., Yoneda, K., & Schreiber, A. J. (2016). Smartwatch-based activity recognition: A machine learning approach. In *Proceedings of the IEEE-EMBS international conference on biomedical and health informatics (BHI)* (pp. 426–429). https://doi.org/10.1109/BHI.2016.7455925
Whittaker, S., Bergman, O., & Clough, P. (2010). Easy on that trigger dad: A study of long term family photo retrieval. *Personal and Ubiquitous Computing, 14*(1), 31–43.
Whittaker, S., Kalnikaite, V., Petrelli, D., Sellen, A. J., Villar, N., Bergman, O., . . . Brockmeier, J. (2012). Socio-technical lifelogging: Deriving design principles for a future proof digital past. *Human-Computer Interaction, 27*, 37–62.
Whittaker, S., Tucker, S., Swampillai, K., & Laban, R. (2008). Design and evaluation of systems to support interaction capture and retrieval. *Personal and Ubiquitous Computing, 12*(3), 197–221. https://doi.org/10.1007/s00779-007-0146-3
Wu, C. -I., James Teng, C. -m., Chen, Y.- C., Lin, T. -Y., Chu, H. -H., & Hsu, J. Y. -j. (2007). Point-of-capture archiving and editing of personal experiences from a mobile device. *Personal and Ubiquitous Computing, 11*(4), 235–249. https://doi.org/10.1007/s00779-006-0082-7
Wu, H., Lemaire, E. D., & Baddour, N. (2012). Activity change-of-state identification using a Blackberry smartphone. *Journal of Medical and Biological Engineering, 32*(4), 265. https://doi.org/10.5405/jmbe.967
Wu, P., Zhu, J., & Zhang, J. Y. (2013). MobiSens: A versatile mobile sensing platform for real-world applications. *Mobile Networks and Applications, 18*(1), 60–80. https://doi.org/10.1007/s11036-012-0422-y
Xie, J. L., Schaubroeck, J., & Lam, S. S. K. (2008). Theories of job stress and the role of traditional values: A longitudinal study in China. *Journal of Applied Psychology, 93*(4), 831–848. https://doi.org/10.1037/0021-9010.93.4.831
Yang, L.-Q., Spector, P. E., Chang, C.-H., Gallant-Roman, M., & Powell, J. (2012). Psychosocial precursors and physical consequences of workplace violence towards nurses: A longitudinal examination with naturally occurring groups in hospital settings. *International Journal of Nursing Studies, 49*(9), 1091–1102. https://doi.org/10.1016/j.ijnurstu.2012.03.006
Zapf, D., Dormann, C., & Frese, M. (1996). Longitudinal studies in organizational stress research: A review of the literature with reference to methodological issues. *Journal of Occupational Health Psychology, 1*(2), 145–169. https://doi.org/10.1037/1076-8998.1.2.145
Zhang, S., McCullagh, P., Nugent, C., & Zheng, H. (2010). Activity monitoring using a smart phone's accelerometer with hierarchical classification. In V. Callaghan (Ed.), *Proceedings of the international conference on intelligent environments* (pp. 158–163). https://doi.org/10.1109/IE.2010.36
Zhang, S., McCullagh, P., Zhang, J., & Yu, T. (2014). A smartphone based real-time daily activity monitoring system. *Cluster Computing, 17*(3), 711–721. https://doi.org/10.1007/s10586-013-0335-y
Zheng, Y. (2015). Human activity recognition based on the hierarchical feature selection and classification framework. *Journal of Electrical and Computer Engineering, 2015*(4), 1–9. https://doi.org/10.1155/2015/140820

MIX
Papier aus verantwortungsvollen Quellen
Paper from responsible sources
FSC® C105338

If you have any concerns about our products,
you can contact us on
ProductSafety@springernature.com

In case Publisher is established outside the EU,
the EU authorized representative is:
Springer Nature Customer Service Center GmbH
Europaplatz 3, 69115 Heidelberg, Germany

Printed by Libri Plureos GmbH
in Hamburg, Germany